Joy and Heartbreak

Struggles in Critical-Needs Schools

Joy and Heartbreak

Struggles in Critical-Needs Schools

Kerry P Holmes
Stacy V Holmes
Jerilou J Moore

Anchor Book Press

Joy and Heartbreak: Struggles in Critical-Needs Schools
Copyright © 2025 Kerry P Holmes, Stacy V Holmes, Jerilou J Moore
Cover images digitally edited by Annie Moore. All images are used under license from shutterstock.com
Imprint: Anchor Book Press
440 W Colfax Street, Unit 1132, Palatine, IL 60078
ISBN: 9781958992296

Printed in the United States

All rights reserved. No part of this publication may be reproduced, stored in a retrieval system, or transmitted in any form by any means without the prior written per-mission of the author.

Table of Contents

INTRODUCTION — 1

CHAPTER 1
AUGUST – FIRST DAYS OF SCHOOL — 5

CHAPTER 2
SEPTEMBER – LAST DAYS OF SUMMER — 43

CHAPTER 3
OCTOBER-NOVEMBER – FALL HAS ARRIVED — 79

CHAPTER 4
DECEMBER-JANUARY – WINTER HOLIDAYS — 117

CHAPTER 5
FEBRUARY-MARCH – MIDDLE OF WINTER — 159

CHAPTER 6
APRIL-MAY – SPRINGTIME — 181

EPILOGUE
FIVE YEARS LATER — 207

REFERENCES — 215

Introduction
By Kerry Holmes

"When did you teach?" This question from a student teacher changed my life! I gave her a vague answer, because it had been several years since I had taught. Steeped in the newest information about teaching as a graduate student, I had been wanting to return to the public-school classroom. This question was the inspiration that drove me back into the classroom in a critical-needs, low-performing elementary school.

    As a rusty old teacher, I would like to invite preservice, beginning, and experienced teachers, and administrators into my first-grade classroom to join me in my adventures through my daily entries presented sequentially throughout the school year. You will read about the joyful moments and the heartbreaking experiences encountered in the classroom, coupled with updated commentaries with the benefit of hindsight that address common issue and problems teachers face today.

    With the exception of cleaning up a few spelling and grammatical errors and eliminating some redundancies, these are the entries I dashed off each night after teaching. I used these entries to vent my feelings and to reflect on the day's events. To maintain privacy, I changed the name of the school and its location as well as the names of all students, colleagues, and administrators.

    After reading the entries, cover to cover, I found I had recorded a wealth of information and insights that might just possibly enlighten anyone who has a stake in the education of our children. The stories told through the entries of the successes of the students will warm your heart as the struggles will break it!

Written in italics, entries, titled, "Inside the Classroom," are loaded with teaching ideas based on my classroom experiences, the ones that worked and the ones that flopped. The Teacher-to-Teacher Commentaries that follow each entry clarify lessons learned in the classroom and include research-based information on topics common to today's teachers. Together, the entries and the commentaries can be used to generate lively discussions in college and university classrooms and preservice and inservice teacher workshops. They can also be used to involve teachers in reflective writing about their experiences in the classroom.

This book can be used as a stand-alone trade book or a companion to a textbook for a number of education classes because it highlights issues and problems that occur across the curriculum in today's classrooms.

The shift for student teachers from a protected and limited student-teaching environment to the real world of teaching in their own classroom is swift and brutal. Unlike other professionals, teachers begin their new job totally alone with their students during most of their working hours. Teachers in similar situations may benefit from knowing they are not alone. The struggles they face are endemic to challenges in today's K-6 classrooms.

> Schools serving minority student populations in schools in high poverty areas have a greater teacher shortage than more affluent schools. Students who attend schools in high poverty areas desperately need well-informed, competent, and caring teachers.

You will note that through the first few months of school, the entries and commentaries have a heavy focus on the conflicting philosophies for teaching reading and the other content areas. During graduate school, I learned that the only accepted way of teaching reading was through whole language where students learned to read by being exposed to whole words in books. Over and over again, I was taught that phonics, the connection of oral speech sounds to written words, taught through direct, explicit instruction would kill students' interest and slow their progress in learning to read. Therefore, I felt anguish each time I veered from the whole language philosophy and taught phonics when I felt whole language was just not enough.

The theme of this book is determination that rings throughout the Inside the Classroom entries. Hopefully, it will be a spark that inspires others to reflect on their own practices, try new ideas, and most of all, never give up on the students!

Chapter 1
August – First Days of School

Inside the Classroom, August 12

This is the first day of school, the day I had been anticipating. My classroom is organized, books in neat rows, pencils sharpened, and a huge cutout of a green worm, friendly looking and cute, adorns the wall near our library center. I have a shelf of games and puzzles set up where the children can easily get to them. Because the desks were not uniform in size or shape, it was not possible to arrange them in groups.. I resorted to placing my desks in rows, but remembered how abhorrent rows of desks were to the more progressive university faculty. What if they visited my room and saw factory-like rows? My husband, who had been by my side the entire time, suggested I put the desks in semicircles. Once in semicircles, the room looked better, not as rigid as the rows of desks.

From 7:30-8:15 the students straggled in. Most looked confident and happy, two were crying. One little boy was crying because he could not find our room. Another child was crying because he thought I was going to "whoop him." Our district allows paddling, something I had not encountered in my previous teaching experiences. I vowed I would never paddle a child, and I intend to honor this vow throughout the school year. I met a few parents, but most of the children came alone or with an older brother or sister. One mother who came with her child told me he had been born with developmental disabilities and as a result has physical problems. His fine motor skills are poor, he walks with an unsteady gait, drools, his nose constantly runs, and his speech is difficult to understand. Because he had been retained in preschool, kindergarten, and first grade, he is older than most of the other children. I looked over the sea of faces and prayed I could live up to their hopes and my expectations. I want so badly for them all to succeed.

At the end of the first assignment, the children crowded around me with their finished work. I realized that I had forgotten to have a place for them to put it. I must take time to teach my children classroom routines and rules. I must also get rid of the small stuff by filling out lists, purchase forms, and other minor, but pesky paperwork after school so it does not get lost, and more importantly, so it does not add to the weight of the duties I face.

The final hurdle came unexpectedly at dismissal. I had stick-on name tags that my mentor, Ms. Miller, had given me for each child. However, boys wearing basketball jerseys lost theirs during the day because the stickers did not adhere well to the slick fabric for long. By the end of the day, even the best of the stickers had become lost or torn making it hard to identify the children by name.

There are three ways for the children to leave school: by bus, by car, and walking. Children leaving with a parent may leave at any time. The others left at three different times, the walkers left first, followed by the early bus riders, and then the late bus riders. Without the benefit of name tags and with an incomprehensible loudspeaker, I had to rely on the children to tell me which group they were in. In my attempt at organization, I had posted little yellow school buses next to the door. Each bus had its number and the names of the children written on it. However, to my horror, buses were not called by number, but by the names of the bus drivers! I had no idea who drove each bus and therefore no idea which bus each child should ride and once again relied on their earnest exclamations.

There is so much to do!!! It is almost overwhelming having so many new tasks in unfamiliar surroundings. Where do we sit in the cafeteria? How do the children get their food? Who cleans the tables? Recess brings more questions. Where do we go and how do we get there? When we went out for recess, my children made a dash to the merry-go-round and were having great fun when another teacher told me that last year a little boy broke his leg on the merry-go round and the children are no longer allowed to play on it.

During this first day, I had been drooled on, sneezed on, hugged by a child who had just picked his nose, and patted by little hands sticky with questionable yucky stuff. The little boy with motor control issues and a constant runny nose, approached me with a big grin accompanied by plenty of mucus and gave me a huge hug. Fortunately, I realized this was a defining moment. The rest of the class was watching to see how I would react. I hugged him back to show him and his classmates that he was a valuable and accepted part of our class. In that fleeting instant I knew I had to accept him and demonstrate that to the class; my clothes and I could be washed at the end of the day.

My feet hurt. I was on them constantly from 6:50 to 4:30 with a 20-minute break for lunch. There is little chance to sit. Though not always easy, I tried to maintain a positive attitude. During the school day I delighted in student successes; at night I beat myself up over my failures.

Once the last of my children left, I sat at my desk reflecting on the day's events. As a new teacher, after a long hiatus from teaching in an elementary school, I wrote suggestions for myself:
1. Write down and learn the names of the bus drivers.
2. Be super organized.
3. Write detailed weekly lesson plans in my planning book and more detailed daily notes from my plans on notebook paper so I can use instructional time wisely.
4. Plan, teach, and model rules and routines students are to follow. Let children help develop the classroom and playground rules. Once the rules are made, write them on a list to post in a prominent place in the classroom.
5. Figure out a place for students to put their completed work and plan productive activities for students who finish their work ahead of the others.
6. Get rid of the small stuff.

> This evening I reflected on the advice from a book, *Teacher and Child* by Dr. Hiam Ginott, who studied the effects of classroom interactions on students. He found that teachers possess tremendous powers over the daily lives of their students. His book contains sage advice for anyone working with students. The following are two brief quotes from his book that will give you an idea of the powerful effect you have on your students:
>
> "I have come to the frightening conclusion that I am the decisive element. I can humiliate or heal."
> "It is my response that decides whether a crisis is escalated or de-escalated, and a person is humanized or dehumanized." (Ginott, 1972, Preface)

Teacher-to-Teacher Commentary

That night, I eagerly began to write my first, of many, journal entries. Reviewing the events of the day was cathartic. Reflections on events and my feelings, good and bad, helped me to determine ways to overcome difficult situations and think of possible approaches to solve problems and help the classroom function more smoothly. Picturing the children in my class as I wrote helped me resolve to be the best teacher I could be for them. Writing about the students entrusted to me helped end the day on a positive note.

Other than buying and wearing more comfortable shoes, I learned that having a written list of procedures and routines clearly thought out for the first day is essential. I must plan my rules, routines, and classroom management strategies as carefully as I plan my lessons for content learning.

My mentor, Ms. Miller, had a form for parents to fill out as they dropped their children off at school that included a space for allergies and medical conditions such as asthma. There should also be a place on the form for parents to give their permission to let substitute teachers know their children's special needs. Because most of my children came with an older sibling or alone, this permission would have to be done through personal contact or written communication.

Corporal punishment, known as paddling, is still allowed in schools in 19 states including Mississippi. In recent years, paddling in Mississippi has been significantly reduced since the 2019 Mississippi law that prohibits the use of corporal punishment on students with a disability and an IEP (Individualized Education Program). Parents have the right to withhold permission for their child to be paddled. Because paddling has shown mixed results for controlling behavior, many school districts are looking toward counseling rather than corporal punishment (ProCon, 2023).

Inside the Classroom, August 13

We are required to turn in our plan book to the principal every Friday and reference our objectives to the benchmarks and competencies of the Mississippi mathematics and language arts standards. Referencing our plans to the standards is an excellent idea, but there are no hard copies to consult and finding them online was difficult because of limited access to computers. However, omission of the standards was never an issue at our school.

Teacher-to-Teacher Commentary

Students at the university would benefit from knowing that the form they are required to use for lesson planning during student teaching is much longer than the ones their clinical instructors (master teachers) are required to use. The clinical instructors wrote in little blocks in a lesson plan book while university students were required to write a two-week lesson plan complete with assessment, procedures, objectives, remediation, and enrichment activities. Referencing the state standards was not required at our school. Instead, we used the standards set forth in the teacher's manuals for reading and mathematics. We did not have textbooks or teacher's manuals for the other content areas. Today, standards-based learning has become widely accepted and accessible. They would have been extremely helpful during the time I taught. Each state and content area has its own set of standards. The standards for Mississippi are available through the Mississippi Updated College and Career-Readiness Standards (2016) for language arts, mathematics, science, social studies, and art. In addition to the standards, there are Scaffolding Documents for English Language Arts and Mathematics to guide teachers in making decisions on the progression of learning their students should follow. Additional standards are offered through each of the content-area organizations found online or they can be purchased as a hard copy.

Inside the Classroom, August 16

The bathroom is already an issue. Today, when I took the entire class at once it took up about 10 minutes of instructional time. When I tried using red and green stop and go passes, there was a steady stream of students jumping up to get a pass. I must enforce a no bathroom rule when I am giving directions. At this point, I think the passes stand the best chance of working though I must teach and reinforce the rules for using them.

With so much instructional time devoted to classroom management, planned bathroom trips, intercom, and in-person interruptions, much of my valuable time is wasted. Nine of my 21 children have been held back, some more than once. I need every possible minute of instructional time. I desperately want them to succeed!!

Otherwise, the morning went well. Everyone worked and there were few behavior problems. This afternoon was less structured during science and social studies and there were numerous minor, but annoying discipline problems. Mostly, the students kept leaving their seats for no reason. I must plan a way to teach them when they can leave their seats and give them more opportunities to move such as stretches, marching to music, and so forth.

I immediately determined that organization is the key to a successful day. Each part of every lesson must be carefully planned with materials organized and ready to use. What has worked well so far is that I plan one week in advance as required by the district. The night before, I review my plans, list the steps for teaching on notebook paper, and write instructional prompts on Post-it notes. This refreshed my memory and the Post-it notes were easy to refer to during the lesson.

It is Friday and I can leave my apartment near the school and drive home! There is so much planning I want to do over the weekend. It is essential to plan activities that continue my drive toward meeting academic objectives.

Teacher-to-Teacher Commentary

After two days of school, my understanding of the importance of organization and planning increased enormously. Though I knew organization and planning were paramount to good teaching and classroom management, my respect for their importance increased one hundred-fold. There are no shortcuts! The first step in planning is to become an expert in the content of the lesson. For example, for the teaching of reading it is necessary to have a firm grasp of the terminology for spoken and written words such as phonemic awareness, phoneme, consonant blend, digraph, and diphthong so you can decide how to order the presentation of these skills in your weekly or even monthly plans.

One way to plan for trouble spots during the day is to visualize your classroom routines such as attendance and lunch choices that must be sent to the office first thing, calendar time, pencil problems, bathroom time, and places for students to put their completed work.

Next, it is important to plan how you will sell the importance of the lessons to your students. My students, many who had been held back one or more years, craved work because they wanted to learn and experience success. However, their behavior often got in the way of the learning they craved.

Blending curriculum goals with pedagogy is challenging. It requires taking multiple functions of the lessons into account such as the needs and behavior of the students, pacing of the lesson, ways to keep and sustain attention, and ordering procedures for each lesson. However, planning does not stop here! Other decisions on when and how to assess students, how to connect the lesson to the students' prior knowledge, types of questions to ask, and making or gathering instructional materials all must be integrated into one lesson.

Inside the Classroom, August 17

After a short week, this was my fourth day of teaching. What a crash course in teaching I am experiencing! Teaching is one long "Whack-a-Mole" game. Just when one is subdued, three more pop up demanding attention. I have another evening of planning and grading to do. This job is exhausting!

The three major problems I face are discipline, dialect, and supplies. Many, but not all, of the parents sent basic supplies with their children. Like most of the teachers, I brought in necessary supplies such as soap and paper towels for the bathroom, facial tissues, extra pencils, crayons, grade-level writing paper, and so forth.

The children, school secretary, and my assistant, Ms. Cook, are still virtually incomprehensible to me. I ask the children and my assistant to repeat what they are saying until I can catch a few words and put together meaning from bits of words and phrases. I just ignore the secretary's interruptions over the loud speaker or ask other teachers whom I can understand. When the children talked to each other, their voices were loud. When they talked to me, they were muffled and hard to understand. More than once a child would come to me and mumble, "Can I use?" Even after I figured out the words, I did not understand the question. What was it they wanted to use? I quickly learned, "Can I use" is short for "Can I use the bathroom." I mentioned this to one of the first-grade teachers. She said she had the same problem and that it took about two weeks for her to understand her students' speech.

Teacher-to-Teacher Commentary

When our family moved from northern Virginia to Mississippi, our children and I had trouble understanding the southern dialect. At the beginning of school, our daughter came home and asked where we got our water. I patiently explained that our water came from city water towers. She then said, "My teacher told me we got our water from "whales." What the teacher was trying to communicate, was that some people get their water from "wells." Another time, a friend said, "Your hair, your hair!" I reached up to smooth my hair, when it occurred to me that our friend was glad to see us and had said, "You're here, you're here!" Misunderstanding language can occur to all people, for a variety of reasons making communicating frustrating and difficult.

Grande (2020) addressed active listening skills and their importance for building relationships. By following some of the steps proposed by Grande such as eye contact, asking questions, and summarizing what students said, I felt confident that within two weeks I would overcome my difficulty with the southern dialect.

The cultural and language differences between teachers who live in a community vastly different from their students can lead to communication problems. For the past four days, I faced numerous communication problems which was ironic because I had made a pledge driving to school on the first day that I would be an active listener for my students. I knew how important it was to share my thoughts with people who were truly listening, and how frustrated I felt when I sensed their mind was on other things.

However, I could not get a handle on what my students were trying to tell me and kept asking them to repeat themselves. The southern dialect came between my ability to be an active listener, necessary to build the relationships I wanted to establish with my students. I know of no convenient dictionary that will resolve the differences in speech across socioeconomic and cultural divides.

In his classic book, originally published in 1812 in England that has endured over time, Samuel Johnson (2023, p. 40) listed five differences in speech. The differences in speech between my children and myself are timeless!

1. Differences in accent,
2. Differences in prosody,
3. Differences in syntax,
4. Differences in grammar, person, number, tense, and case,
5. Differences in usage.

Young children learn to talk by imitating the speech around them. Because I grew up in California, I found that the speech spoken around me did not carry the same accent or even the same expressions as people living in the South. Children have a way of blurting out messages out of context and their utterances were often incomplete sentences that I could not understand because of their pronunciation.

Communities have their own speech patterns and local jargon. Within the community of the school, students adopt the words and pronunciation from their homes and their peers. Often these speech patterns are engrained in speech through repeated exposures and other times they are deliberate attempts to fit in with peers or to emulate gangs. Yes, gang influence begins early. Some of my children began to draw and color intricate designs which they gave me and in return, received lots of praise. Two of my reliable students told me that the designs were a gang symbol. I put an immediate stop to making gang symbols and explained why. How sad for the children, and how naïve of me.

The names of Black children often reflect their cultural background. They are frequently based on African, Muslim, and Creole names (Waugaman, 2015). Though the names of the children who appear in the entries have been changed, I duplicated some of the common patterns in the names I chose to replace.

Inside the Classroom, August 18

I feel exhausted, inadequate, stressed, and excited, a panoply of emotions. Can I really do this? These were the thoughts I wrote in my journal toward the end of my first full week teaching. Planning takes so much time. I feel a real pull to the textbook manuals. They provide order, structure, and activities for each lesson. This is hard to reconcile with the constructivist approach I had been learning and teaching at the university. The university approach requires materials and time for students to explore learning in their own way. The teacher's role is to encourage and guide the students as they learn from their experiences.

At this point the children do not even keep pencils at their desks. Upon the advice of my mentor, I collect all pencils after my students have completed their assignment to prevent them from playing with them, and in some cases totally destroying them by pulling off the erasers, breaking the lead, and peeling back the wood. I need to ease into allowing students the responsibility of keeping their own pencils. I must take notes on events that trigger misbehavior for each of my students and plan a task analysis of the lessons I teach to gather data on the things that worked and the things that did not work. This information will guide my planning and point me in the right direction for possible behavioral problems and ways to help students work through them.

Teacher-to-Teacher Commentary

Teacher modeling is a useful tool when you explicitly demonstrate aspects of classroom behavior and social skills. Think aloud and use positive and negative examples to help your students understand your expectations. Before determining how to model desired behaviors and academic outcomes, visualize the problem areas you think students might encounter. As you model, verbalize your thinking as you show students what to do. Continue to think of possible common errors and expected problems that will frustrate students. This verbalized show and tell can include difficulties and even deliberate mistakes to let your students understand that these pesky problems are a part of learning. Modeling can be interactive when you invite students to demonstrate or narrate how they completed a task or solved a problem. The common saying, "I do, we do, you do" is a popular approach that summarizes modeling.

Inside the Classroom, August 19

Upon reading the cumulative files of my children, the thing that stood out to me was that behavior was marked low for almost all of the children assigned to my class. Nine of my 21 students had been retained at least once. After substitute teaching in critical-needs elementary and high school in Virginia, I felt confident I could control the behavior of my students, I was in for a bit of a surprise!

Many of the teachers who had had my students in their classrooms freely offered unwelcome comments about them. Though I had a general idea about the histories of the students, I wanted the students to begin their year with a fresh start. Helpful information on behavioral strategies that worked would have been welcome, but general negative comments were NOT welcome.

Aside from behavioral issues, another major problem is the effect constant interruptions have on instructional time. In my quest to help my students learn, and be promoted to the next grade, I value my instructional time over all else. We were told by our principal, Ms. Wrigley, that intercom interruptions take away 12 minutes of instructional time each time our room is called and plans to use **walky-talkies** *to cut down on the interruptions. Here is what happens when the intercom clicks on. We all become quiet so we can hear a message that usually does not apply to our class. For example, ten minutes before I had to get my children ready to go home, the secretary called over the intercom and asked me to send "cluckle seck crick to stookle pops clack." I asked the teacher across the hall what the secretary said and she did not know either, so I ignored the garbled message thinking that if it were important, she would call again.*

Teacher-to-Teacher Commentary

Reading the cumulative folders to learn about my students was helpful. They contained information on the students in my class in a nonjudgmental way. The information just reported facts that will help me know the strengths and weaknesses of my students.

Because so many of my students had been retained, some multiple times, the teachers who had taught them in prior years may have meant well, but their unsolicited comments were not helpful. These teachers could not provide me with the nuances to the students' behavior they experienced in their classrooms. Instead, they simply expressed frustration and sometimes horror, an "ain't it awful," attitude toward the behavior of many of the students assigned to my class. Frankly, I resented empty negative comments made about the children I was just getting to know.

Instructional time is such a valuable commodity. Imagine how long it takes a teacher, in the middle of a lesson who is interrupted by an announcement over the school-wide intercom to listen to the message, determine whether it applies to the class, and then try to re-focus the 21 students, who were also listening to the speaker get back to the lesson. Think of the time wasted if it happens 10 times a day. Using the 12-minute time our principal told us each intercom announcement took, that is 120 minutes, two hours of wasted instructional time. If the intercom is crackling and noisy, it just makes it worse. The issue of crackling and noisy intercoms, however, isn't the root of the problem. The problem is the lack of discipline on the part of office personnel. They simply shouldn't interrupt multiple classrooms for a single student. They should send a messenger.

Inside the Classroom, August 20

With active students, the semicircle arrangement of desks lasted less than a day. By the end of the day the desks were not in any order. They are now in rows. I had worked to arrange my classroom in a way that enabled me to involve my students in methods supported by the constructivist approach. I was going to be the facilitator of learning while the children worked together to learn through exploration, collaboration and problem solving. Tables facilitated this approach, while desks in a row were frowned upon as an old-fashioned stratey that isolated the children from each other.

Having just come from the university, my mind was filled with all the wonderful ways I could teach my students through setting up a constructivist-centered classroom. I keenly felt the battle between two competing approaches for teaching reading:
> *1. Direct instruction where lessons are sequenced around specific objectives directed by the teacher.*
> *2. Constructivism where students work together to construct knowledge from their experiences facilitated by the teacher.*

These two different approaches reminded me of the grinning Cheshire Cat in the story, "Alice in Wonderland" where during a walk in the woods, Alice must choose one of two routes. When she asked the grinning Cheshire Cat for advice, he asked, "Where are you going?" Alice replied, "I don't know." The grinning cat wisely responded, "Well, if you don't know where you are going, any road will do very nicely."

I know the constructivist philosophy was embraced by my colleagues in the School of Education, yet the phonics method makes sense and has a growing body of research to support it. Where is the Cheshire cat when I need him?

I created work folders that included multiple activities for my children to work on while others were finishing their work. They chose the ones they wanted to do. The activities contained interesting fiction and nonfiction reading passages, crossword and word search puzzles, and easy beginner sudoku puzzles. I plan to vary the activities to match their interests and my learning objectives. These activities further learning far more than having my students sit quietly, color pictures on a worksheet, or put their heads down until the others finished their work.

Teacher-to-Teacher Commentary

No debate has ripped apart our educational system as much as the debate over whether constructivism or direct instruction is the best way to teach children. Many teachers and administrators have staked out positions from which they refuse to budge. Schools of Education were not immune from this debate. They too have chosen sides, almost always embracing the progressive philosophy underlying constructivism. This ideological position was then transmitted to preservice teachers who have a hard time, as I did, reconciling a single view with the real world of their classrooms.

Teachers are guided by their philosophy of education. Some have a well-articulated set of beliefs based on knowledge and reflection while others are guided by a weaker set of beliefs. Teachers who have a weak belief system fall prey to the whims of others or wander aimlessly toward an uncertain destination.

Constructivism, the philosophy that students learn more when constructing information for themselves when given time and materials, rather than receiving it from others became popular in the 1960s. Constructivism became part of the philosophy of the Whole Language movement in the 1980's and 1990's. Popular slogans were, "Marinate your children in books," and "Teachers just have to get out of the way and let students read." If only it were that easy!

My attempts to create a constructivist classroom environment were based on what I learned through my university classes and the philosophies held by the professors, yet my first-grade students worked harder and learned more through a well-structured teacher-taught lesson. My Cheshire Cat moment of choosing one road did not work for me. I needed to travel both roads, maximum exposure to books and direct instruction on word decoding, to reach my destination, student learning.

The years I was away from the elementary classroom saw a philosophical shift toward progressive constructivist ideals based on the erroneous fact that children learned to read as naturally as they learned to talk. This romantic ideal to teach children to read through exposure to multiple encounters with written words had replaced the direct teaching of phonics where children learned to connect spoken sounds to written letters, letter patterns, and syllables with skills being taught explicitly.

Constructivism continued to be the preferred approach despite the growing body of scientific research that eventually led to the Reading Wars between phonics instruction and whole language where students could read books using word configuration, comprehension cues, and repetitious exposure to print. I sought to embrace constructivism whenever I could. I used the whole word method that embraced reading repetitive words in textbooks. I had my students rely on pictures and word configuration where they outlined the shape of the word to see the word as a complete unit rather than the individual letters within the shape. Today, word configuration, known as the word-shape model, is not supported by research because it does not help children recognize and use their knowledge of the letters and the sounds they represent within the word (Basit et al 2023).

I found, with my student population it was important to try a variety of direct instruction and constructivist-based approaches to promote the learning of basic skills. Come to think of it, isn't the constructing of words from the individual speech sounds (phonics) in line with the constructivist approach?

Inside the Classroom, August 23

On the first day of school, the students were on their best behavior. As they began to settle in, disruptive behaviors began to surface from some of the students. Little things like dropping pencils, talking, leaving their seats, and interrupting during a lesson began to happen. It reminded me of a day I substituted in a third-grade class in a critical-needs school in Virginia. At the beginning of the day, a little girl looked at me and deliberately pushed her desk over spilling the contents. With the class watching, I approached the girl and told her I was sorry her desk "fell over" and bent down to help her pick up her belongings. During this time, I asked her little questions such as, "Do you have a pet?" or, "What do you like to do after school?" She began responding and sat back at her desk and never posed another discipline problem during the rest of the class. I need to come up with basic and creative ways to defuse behavior problems in my class.

Classroom management is the number one concern with the first-year teachers I have met. Now I have the same concern. I have as my primary focus establishing classroom behavior and routines. I need quiet and order when I am teaching so

---

Rather than adhering strictly to one theory or another, teachers should strive to have what Stanovich (2000) calls, "what works epistemologies." He points out that like the best scientists, the best teachers should not be constrained by a single ideology; they should be "opportunistic practitioners seizing on methods that work." Stanovich (2000, p.

I am very strict about the children's behavior, yet my attempts to get and keep their attention are short-lived. Even the quiet students are often focused on pulling loose threads from their socks or pushing eraser bits around on their desks.

I have been striving to create a constructivist classroom where the children interact with each other and have hands-on authentic experiences. I am now firmly convinced with my population, poor, rural, and Black, that I must strive toward the goals that promote responsibility and collaboration with others. However, the children at this point are unable to handle much freedom.

Teacher-to-Teacher Commentary

Classroom management of student behavior is a serious challenge to teachers. It may come as a surprise when first-time new teachers get their own classroom of 20-25 students. Teachers, unlike other professionals, have lived through the experiences of the classroom beginning in preschool and extending through higher education. Many have played school using dolls, stuffed animals, and willing adults. Such familiar experiences initially led many, including the authors, to believe teaching is fun, teaching comes naturally. We have filtered out of our memories, the hard work of the teachers who had to plan lessons, deal with unruly students, gather materials, and start each day with a warm welcome and a smile, despite what was going on in their personal lives.

In preparation for becoming a teacher, university students have had plenty of hands-on classroom experiences through field experiences in public schools where the teacher and frequently their university instructor, were present when they taught. During these times, the elementary students presented far fewer discipline problems. Teacher candidates did not have to consider the serious work of addressing discipline problems as the groundwork had already been laid by the teachers.

Along with the challenges of teaching academics and social skills, teachers must compete with a myriad of serious behaviors. Too many teachers are leaving the classroom because they have become exhausted and disillusioned from dealing with bad student behavior that has escalated over the years. Problems such as fighting, interrupting lessons, and ignoring directions are now common (Lambert, 2022).

> The statistics on disillusioned teachers speak for themselves. According to the U.S. Bureau of Labor and Statistics (Torpey, 2018), the number of elementary teachers who quit in the middle or at the end of their first year is estimated to be on average 100,000 from 2016 through 2026. A total of 48,300 leave the teaching profession entirely. The rest simply transfer to another teaching job.

Before the Covid pandemic, Morrison (2019) reported that nation-wide, more teachers quit after their first year than at any other time in the last 20 years. Critical-needs schools suffered an even larger turnover of teachers. Many teachers who chose to work in a poor performing school had their high expectations dashed by the realities of the surrounding community and within the school.

The exodus from the classroom was worsened by the 2020 Covid 19 pandemic. According to a report from Rand Publishers, the pandemic was responsible for almost half the teachers who voluntarily left the public schools to seek different jobs saying stress was the reason (Dilberti, Schwartz, & Grant, 2021).

In our own experiences, we have personally known first year teachers in low and high-performing schools who quit in the middle or at the end of the school year. All left because of discipline. They no longer wanted to play the Whack-a-Mole game. Goodwin, (2012) found that behavior was the top reason teachers left the classroom. He quoted an Australian first-year teacher who said, "I don't have the professional skills to deal with this extreme behavior."

Inside the Classroom, August 24

This is my tenth day of teaching. I continue to feel stressed, but also excited about helping my students learn. I want to do more progressive child-centered activities, but I must ease into them rather than jump into them.. My children are slowly acquiring the skills to join a center quietly, take turns, and work together. The centers must be simple. Very well planned and organized. Appropriate behavior must be taught and monitored. Lots of modeling helped.

Having all materials ready with a CLEAR idea of how they will be used is essential. Murky planning such as "The children will play the game Go Fish using math cards with numerals and number words" did not go smoothly and we stopped. Murky planning led to problems such as the cards were not shuffled well and I did not have equal sets for all children. This game has possibilities, but next time I will be better prepared. Instead, I substituted another activity for the game of Go Fish. My children sat at their desks and copied number words from the board. They loved it!!! Some did not want to stop writing when it was time for recess. That is hard to figure out. Perhaps the clear sense of purpose with a tangible end product was appealing.

Teacher-to-Teacher Commentary

When you are stressed, try laughter! Laughter creates mental and physical changes that are mood changing for teachers and their students (Mayo Clinic, 2021). If you think this is just another fad, try it! Laugh and feel the physical and mental changes that occur within your own body. Laugh at yourself and funny things that happen in the classroom. A jolly sense of humor can go a long way toward maintaining students' interest in the lessons. Just be sure your laughter does not embarrass or shame any of the students.

To manufacture laughable moments, you can find a myriad of corny jokes such as, "Why did the frog cross the road?'(Answer: "To get to the other side.") Knock-knock jokes are aways fun such as, "Knock, knock." Students respond, "Who's there?" Teacher says, "Boo." Students say, "Boo who?" Teacher says, "You don't have to cry about it!" Students can make up their own knock-knock jokes to tell the class.

Mad Libs is a word game that combines comprehension, vocabulary, and grammar in a hilarious interactive activity. Ask students to supply a noun, verb, adjective, or adverb. Fill in their suggestions to generate a funny story. Mad Libs are based on themes that include popular children's books. They can be used for a class break or a reading and grammar lesson. In our experience, we have found them to be a favorite of students of all ages. Mad Libs can be found in stores and online.

My entries throughout the school year show how I tried to live up to the widely accepted and highly touted progressive constructivist philosophy of teaching. However, my students preferred the more structured approach that I frequently used. In hindsight, I would still use centers where students are free to explore, but structure their activities to meet specific learning goals. These goals would give students purpose for their center activities and guide them to think through the actions they take. For example, for the Science "I Wonder…" table, I provided magnifying glasses for students to explore the insects, plant life, and soil and rocks they brought in from the playground and encouraged them to study the items, draw a picture, and write a label or brief description of what they learned. This would have been a much more productive center if I had written learning goals such as: Determine why a spider is called an arachnid rather than an insect. Identify the parts of an insect. Sort the number of different particles you found in a cup of dirt and determine where they could have come from. With guidance, students would go beyond casually handling and glancing at the items on the science table to inquiring and learning facts about them. Even with Lego building blocks, one of the most popular centers, I could have moved learning beyond playful exploration to physics, engineering, and mathematics concepts. I could have challenged students by asking how many more Legos would they need to build a tower three feet high. Or, by asking "how to questions" such as how to build a solid structure, how to build a bridge high enough for a large truck to go under, how to test the strength of their bridge, how to determine ways to strengthen their bridge, how to design and build a structure with moving parts, and so many other possibilities (Holmes, Moore, & Holmes, (2023).

Inside the Classroom, August 25

Teachers are very free with their comments about other children. So far, the horror stories or grand pronouncements such as, "Oh you have Julious! I just couldn't stand him!" do not match my images of my students. No one is as bad as I have been told. Additionally, these children are now my students and they are often delightful. If I am sternly lecturing them on some aspect of behavior and a child makes a comical comment, I just have to laugh in spite of myself. Julious then tells me he just loves it when I laugh. How can anyone not love these children? Constructive or useful comments from other teachers would be helpful, but I take unsolicited negative comments with a grain of salt.

I find that all I think about and talk about are the children in my class, my successes and failures, the cute things they did, and the not-so-cute things they did. It does not matter what I am doing, unbidden thoughts enter my head. Through these thoughts, I have come up with some neat insights and ideas.

I came to this job as a first-grade teacher top heavy in theory. My prior teaching experience was too long ago to be of much help to me now. My knowledge and beliefs in education are being harshly tested. When I took a class at the university and I did not do well, I failed. Now, if I do not do well, my students fail. This is a very heavy responsibility, and accounts for most of the stress I am feeling.

At the end of the very first day of class my students stunned me by asking for their homework. When I smiled sweetly and told them there was no homework that day, they looked crestfallen, not happy. They wanted homework! I quickly gave out a simple math worksheet and I could hardly believe my ears when they thanked me for it. Through this experience, I learned to plan homework. What is appropriate homework? It must be self-explanatory for I have been told that some parents do not read well or are too busy with work to help. All my ideas of "meaningful homework" must be rethought. Though family projects are not out of the question, I must assign simple worksheets on important concepts that the children can work on alone.

I am fully aware that for most of my children this is a do-or-die year. Many have repeated first grade and are already very concerned whether they are passing. I never want to plan homework that will simply keep them busy. Carefully planned homework is a way to build in success for students who have previously failed. So far, all children are receiving good grades on their homework because the work is simple review. It is important to build on what they already know.

Homework provides a way to promote responsibility. My students have done a good job turning in their homework folder first thing in the morning on a specific spot on a specific table near my desk. If all directions were followed, they received a sticker on their folder. The sticker was unrelated to the quality of work within the folder, it was only to reward students for remembering to bring in their folders from home and follow directions for returning them to the right place. Of course, I graded the homework giving my children earned stars and stickers along with plenty of positive written feedback. I loved to see them work to read the little notes I wrote to them. They were so interested in reading what I wrote that they consulted each other to decipher the words I had written on their paper.

Teacher-to-Teacher Commentary

This quote that I came across from a six-year-old student should help all of us keep our learning expectations high: "My teacher thought I was smarter than I was, so I was!"

Teachers' negative comments can have a profound effect on a student's self-image. The teachers who spoke to me, did not speak privately, but in the hallway in front of a lot of students. Some of the students could have easily heard and passed along the message to the child under attack. The statement, "I couldn't stand him," said it all. A year in a classroom where a child was likely ignored, belittled, and humiliated is bound to have lasting effects on confidence and achievement.

The homework debate has been going on for a century with no definite conclusion in sight. Some researchers say homework, when done correctly, helps students. Others say that no homework is the best homework. Drew (2023) enumerated 27 "Top Homework Pros and Cons" while another author promoted the idea of "balanced" homework (Terada, 2015) as if someone were advocating "unbalanced" homework.

The common rule of thumb for time spent on homework is and has been 10 minutes times the grade of the student. That is, the literature says that a first grader should get (10 x 1 = 10) ten minutes of homework. Taken literally, that would suggest that sixth graders ought to get 60 minutes and so forth. Overall commentary by researchers Cooper, Robinson, and Patall (2006) always seems to assume that homework, from the students' standpoint, is bad.

That's not the attitude my students displayed. Instead, my students felt proud when they turned in homework, and few failed to do so. Whether it was perfect, mediocre, or poor, they wanted to bring me a product of their labors. They were upset when I inadvertently denied them that opportunity.

A blog from University of the People (2023) provides updated information on the homework debate. It would seem that many of the cons reported by Cooper, Robinson, and Patall (2006) lack context. For instance, homework only encourages a sedentary lifestyle if the assigned work is itself, sedentary, work sheets, for example. But we can think of literally hundreds of examples of homework that require purposeful movement, both outside in the open air and inside the house. So can you. Of course, homework in hostile homes "isn't healthy," but that's not the fault of the homework. Furthermore, although listed as a con, it adds to a "full-time" job. We need to consider what's the alternative activity if students do not have homework? Screen time?

Pros and Cons of Homework	
Pros	**Cons**
Homework:	Homework:
Encourages practice	Encourages sedentary lifestyle
Gets parents involved	Unhealthy in some homes
Teaches time management	Adds to full-time job
Opens communication	Sometimes doesn't get results
Permits more learning time	Sometimes is overdone
Reduces screen time	

Cooper, Robinson, and Patall (2006)

One real difficulty with homework that is not listed above should be mentioned. When determining the homework assignment, the teacher should assume that many children are working alone, that is, they are not receiving any instruction while completing the assignment. So, the directions should be specific and in-depth with a clearly stated goal so that the child, at home, is not left at sea without a clue. The frustration that comes with the lack of understandable instructions can certainly be an ingredient that destroys the purpose of the assignment.

Inside the Classroom, August 26

Giving students responsibility is easier said than done with the students in my class. My students crave structure over open-ended learning. Whoever said that textbooks were the antithesis of a constructivist classroom? Even with the more structured approach, I am able to add in lots of writing, multisensory activities, and group work, but the scope and sequence of my lessons are determined by my learning objectives.

After a few days of writing, my children, who had been reluctant to write, were able to compose two or three sentences using invented and conventional spelling. Obviously, some wrote fewer words than others. However, I am very encouraged. So far, the handwriting program I am using from "The Writing Road to Reading" (Spalding & Spalding, 1990) is working for the children. The children are able to write many letters very neatly, except for De'Andre, the little boy with physical problems, who is still struggling. However, even he is able to write letters that are legible, if not neat.

My children are making progress. I had just read to them the classic tale of "Peter Rabbit" written by Beatrix Potter where Peter, a naughty little rabbit, almost got caught by Mr. McGregor and made into rabbit pie. After discussing the story, I asked them for words they thought they would need to write about Peter Rabbit. I wrote each of their suggestions on the board along with a few that I thought should be included. At first many of my children simply copied the words I had written on the board in no particular order. At this point, with just a few letters and the sounds the letters represent under their belts, they were fearful to sound out the word or even to write the first sound of the word. Still, I told them to write any letters they thought would be in the word (an invented spelling strategy). Interestingly, my students resisted invented spelling as they wanted to spell all their words correctly.

Teacher-to-Teacher Commentary

As I read the log of my experiences after I left the classroom, I know I had plenty of flexibility for teaching my students essential knowledge and skills. The goals of my lessons were not in doubt. It was the tug-of-war between the constructivist approach where I was to provide books and materials to facilitate learning as the children explored and discovered knowledge and the much-maligned direct instruction. Through direct instruction, I was careful to plan my lessons using a series of steps that first attracted students' interest and ended with independent practice. From my years at the university, I was steeped in the idea that the children were eager to learn and all we had to do was put some thought into creating a *writing center, math center* or a *science center* and their natural curiosity would do the rest. But that's not what I found in my classroom.

The children were eager to learn, but they also loved structure, the kind of structure that said, "First we're going to do x and then we are going to do y." That's hardly what the constructivist or discovery point of view suggests. I came to the conclusion that the teacher is often the one with the big ideas on how to offer the students multiple ways to learn the material, but the students must be told the learning objective and understand the steps they are about to pursue to reach it. We can have flexibility on the teacher's part, but structure on the student's part. For example, in a unit on rabbits, teachers can offer the students multiple paths to master the information. They can include lecture, hands-on experiences, technology-based imagery, and written narratives. The teacher can plan these experiences, but the students must follow the paths to knowledge. Anything else was viewed by my students as a social hour.

Invented spelling, sometimes called temporary spelling, is the first developmental stage where students write words according to how they think they sound.

Common errors included words such as "wz" for "was," "no" for "know," "prpl" for "purple." Their early spelling attempts revealed their level of phonics proficiency that provided a good basis to determine which letters to teach or review. As the school year progressed, my students learned more vowel and consonant sounds, how the silent "e" at the end of words can change the vowel sound within the word such as "make," digraphs that represent one sound such as "th," as in "the," and diphthongs, when two vowel sounds are contained in one syllable such as "ow" in "cow" and "oy" in "boy."

When my students recognized that the way they attempted to spell a word did not look right, they wanted to know the correct spelling of the words they wrote right away! To this day, I am not sure I made the right choice, but I supplied the correct spelling when my students asked. I wanted them to keep the flow of their thoughts moving and use their knowledge of phonics by using invented spelling. I did not want spelling to interfere with the joy writing can bring.

Inside the Classroom, August 27

Twelve days of school are now completed. I am beginning to think I can survive and even enjoy this school year, a big improvement over last week when I struggled to get through each day. There are not nearly so many new things to learn and master. I can take roll easily; I know how to dismiss the walkers and the early and late bus riders. Recess duty is almost pleasant. I must copiously plan my lessons being very clear as to what I want the students to learn and how I can best teach them. Sloppy planning, ambiguous directions, and lack of organization of supplies lead to trouble.

I teach a very structured hour and forty-five-minute phonics, writing, and reading lesson in the morning. This time is broken up by a ten-minute bathroom break and one or two breaks of singing or movement. I bought a program, Hooked on Phonics, at a garage sale. It combines singing with movement and my children loved it. Some lessons are available on YouTube and are worth exploring for your beginning or struggling students.

Today the children marched around the room stepping on alphabet tiles saying the sounds for the letters and they loved it! However, the quality of the learning was lower. Many forgot why they were marching, but all were invigorated and participated. I had few, if any, discipline problems during this time. Is the quality of the work reflected in my lesson plans as good in the afternoon as it is for the morning? Though I use direct instruction, I combine it with hands-on activities and group work.

The children are like little sponges. They are eager for knowledge and readily respond. Before showing the video, "Alexander and the Terrible, Horrible, No Good, Very Bad Day," I showed them where Australia is on the world map. In the story, Alexander threatens to move to Australia if his day does not improve. When the word Australia was mentioned in the video all the children turned to look at me and smiled. It was as if we shared some wonderful secret; we knew the location of Australia!

I have tried to give my children more freedom to pursue activities of their choice within the reading, writing, and math centers. We made a modicum of progress today, but the road is long. I must do a task analysis of what it takes to participate and learn independently from a center. Then I must model the behavior and let the children practice, keeping my short-term expectations realistically lower than my vision for my long-term expectations. It may take baby steps to meet my vision, but it is only August, perhaps I have time.

Teacher-to-Teacher Commentary

I firmly believe that a good curriculum consists of a combination of teacher-directed and constructivist learning opportunities. My advice to new and old teachers alike is to search for the best ways to work toward their goals, and never give up.

Though I had plenty of rough spots as a new teacher, learning the rules and routines of the school took a load off me. Perhaps there is a lesson here. If learning the school routines provided comfort and security for me, shouldn't students experience the same feelings of comfort and security after they learned the rules and routines of the classroom? I found that they did. If I skipped a routine, I heard about it from my students.

Every morning, our classroom routine began with saying the Pledge of Allegiance, singing "My Country Tis of Thee," and listening to messages over the intercom. Afterwards, we used the calendar to work on reading, math, science and social studies concepts. During this time, I used phonics to analyze and read the names of the days and the month. We read and compared numbers, worked on number order, and counted the days that have already passed by ones and tens. Students described the weather and made predictions based on the amount of sunlight, clouds, and types of precipitation they saw from the window. Students recognized important dates for the birthdays of important people and historical events. Because my students learned to expect these routine activities on a daily basis, I had few behavioral problems.

Speaking of behavior, routines for behavior should also be an integral part of your routines and content area lesson planning. The times I did not plan the routines for my students to follow were the times I had the most behavioral problems during my lesson. It is easy to miss planning behavioral routines, but they must be a crucial part of each lesson. Think about the routines you want your students to follow at the start of the lesson such as sitting straight, placing their pencil, paper, and book on top of their desk, and waiting quietly for the lesson to begin. These behaviors must be consistently taught and followed with lots of positive feedback. See the January 24 Teacher-to Teacher Commentary for a brief description of the behavioral expectations in China. You will find them interesting.

Inside the Classroom, August 30

The atmosphere in the hallways and classroom is often hostile, at least to my ears. Here are a couple of comments I heard teachers and assistants say today: "Don't act like no kindergartner, act like a grown woman." This was said by a teaching assistant to a kindergarten child during the time the class was standing in line waiting to go to breakfast. Another comment made during the time the children were standing in line waiting for lunch was, "You keep acting like this and you will be out of my life." Another teacher paddles her students for every math problem they get wrong and has received praise by the principal, Ms. Wrigley.

To create a sense of pride and belonging within our class, I told my children that our class should have a name, just like sports teams have a name. We talked about how we could honor our name through all the good things that happen in our class. After much discussion and a vote, our class is now called, "The Tigers." I plan to spend some time on reinforcing how special our class is by referring to it in complimentary ways, such as the "The Tigers work hard!"

Daily, I feel challenged to set up my classroom and plan my lessons based on the progressive philosophy of teaching that I learned in graduate school and taught at the School of Education. However, since entering the classroom as a first-grade teacher, I found that choosing a single approach to teaching does not meet the needs of all my children.

I have come to believe that the whole language philosophy for learning to read must be supported by the direct instruction of phonics. A down side of the constructivist approach is the time it takes to implement activities. For the perfectly normal well-behaved class, the teacher can proceed full speed ahead in creating constructivist lessons complete with exploration and collaborative learning. After listening to teachers in other critical-needs schools, low achieving students learning basic facts cannot easily handle freedom. Many times, my students told me, "We want to do work." Perhaps they go off task when they do not see the value in what they are doing.

The children are less disruptive, have to use the bathroom less frequently, and seem happier when I dictate sentences for them to write or have them work step-by-step mathematics problems. When I try to implement more progressive practices such as group work, paired work, and centers where the children explore and work at their own pace, I am faced with numerous discipline problems. Perhaps the less structured time is perceived as play, not work, and they do not take it as seriously, thinking of it as a social time. They are happiest when they are told what to do and have specific tasks. I am trying to ease them into working independently without as much direction from me.

Teacher-to-Teacher Commentary

You may wonder why the Inside the Classroom entries and Teacher-to-Teacher Commentaries frequently address the dilemma of the methods I used in my classroom. This is due to the consistent hostile treatment of direct instruction by my professors and colleagues that threw me into confusion during my experiences with my first-grade students. When I accompanied a colleague to a reading conference, we went to a session on the direct instruction of phonics. She left after just a few minutes saying, "This is making me sick." and walked out. She was not interested in the science of reading and was devoted to the popular assumption that learning to read comes naturally to children. For her there is a right way and a wrong way to teach and direct instruction is the wrong way!

The reason I continue to be perplexed about the harsh feelings for one philosophy or method than another is that constructivism and direct instruction both offer opportunities for students to learn through active engagement, multisensory lessons, and making connections between new and prior knowledge and experiences. My advice is to use everything you have to help your students learn! I was guided by a long-ago quotation from Engelmann cited in a current article from the National Association of Direct Instruction (2024, p. 1), "If a student fails to learn, it is not the fault of the student, rather the instruction."

It is easy to connect the effects of the negative atmosphere in the classroom and the halls experienced by the children on a daily basis to the experience of dining in a restaurant. Noise combined with an uncomfortable atmosphere, and poor service can kill the dining experience, and, most likely, you will not come back. However, the students have to come back and have to walk in the halls and return to their classrooms. They have no choice. School should be an inviting place where students feel welcome and comfortable.

> At a district meeting, one presenter said something I will never forget, "Don't let children leave one dark place for another."
>
> Children who hear negative comments, criticism, and ridicule at home should not get another dose at school. Tragically, they often do.

Just recently, I learned that one teacher had her students name the rows or tables where they sat with a special name. I wish I had thought of this. I could have referred to the group names for the rows in my classroom setting up a competition among the groups for good behavior and hard work. A study of 1,479 rural and urban classrooms in Chinese primary schools showed mixed results of competition on academic learning (Li, Li, Wu, & Zhen, 2022). We all know that behavior is an enormous factor on academic learning. Negative effects from the Chinese study showed that during competition, the anxiety on students' emotional states interfered with engagement (behavior) and achievement (academics). The advantages were that students experienced pride and were fully engaged, traits necessary to promote good behavior and academic achievement. Though the study was on academic achievement, the students involved in competition first had to control their behaviors of attention, participation, and following the rules.

Naming rows and tables to set up a competition includes an added benefit where the high achievers could serve as good role models for behavior and academic learning. Even after considering the pros and cons of competition and considering the pitfalls and benefits, I wish I had tried it!

Chapter 2
September – Last Days of Summer

Inside the Classroom, September 1

A few of my children like to taste everything in the classroom. If they are near a wall, some like to lick it. Books, pencils, papers all make it to my children's mouths. One child even licked the computer screen. Is this some nutritional deficiency?

Today was a fair day. We got through the plans, I was not too harsh, but there was no real joy or fun. It takes so long to instruct the children on how to turn in papers, wait for them to put down their pencils, wait for all to keep their eyes on me while I am talking, and keep their heads off their desks that much of my instructional time is used up getting the children ready to learn. If I relax my standards, the class quickly disintegrates into a quiet chaos. No one student is doing anything too terribly wrong, but collectively there is an undertone of tapping pencils, tapping feet, audible yawns that are catching if allowed to go unchecked. I must stop repeating directions. The children will come to expect it. I am not sure how to make the children respond the first or second time I say something. Clarifying directions is one thing; repeating directions is another.

To combat signs of boredom, I have been trying to add more fun to our lessons. I went into this job with the idea that everything we did would further the children's academic skills, skills they need to be promoted out of first grade. As much as possible I make skills-based learning meaningful by using authentic items and examples that relate directly to the children's lives. With about half my class performing at the lowest level, I am determined to find ways to overcome behavior problems so my children can learn.

Teacher-to-Teacher Commentary

Research in an article by Lama (2019) may have answered my question about whether licking things is a sign of a nutritional deficiency. Apparently, it could be as simple as the need to explore through the tactile experience of touch. However, by the time children are in school, they should have outgrown the infant and toddler stage of putting everything in their mouths. The name for the condition of tasting and licking things that are nonedible by older children is "pica." Depending on what they taste, pica can lead to health problems if they ingest lead and other toxins. If this condition continues it is important to communicate with parents. For some students it may be a way of coping with stress or seeking attention.

Students' inattention could be due to the pacing of the lesson. Pacing the amount of time students are required to pay attention at any one time, is critical for keeping their attention. A middle school reading teacher in Massachusetts structured a 45-minute read-aloud session into three 15-minute chunks to keep her students engaged. For the first 15 minutes she briefly introduced or reviewed the plot with the students. During this time, they could ask questions and make predictions. For the next 15 minutes, she read to her students, and during the last 15 minutes, she asked high-level questions about the story. The amount of time for each of the three parts to the reading lesson for younger students could be reduced or changed if necessary. To make sure the students were engaged in all three parts of her lesson, she chose high-interest grade-level appropriate books using *The Read-Aloud Handbook* by Trelease & Giorgis. Other excellent sources for selecting high-interest books are the school and community libraries.

When students misbehave, they may be trying to communicate a message to their teacher, or to impress their classmates. The following are a few ways to build a trusting environment where punitive measurements are substituted by positive approaches to misbehavior:

1. Seek underlying causes to behavioral problems. Is the student frustrated because the material is too hard or too lengthy? Is he or she hungry or sick?
2. Intervene early to preempt behavior from worsening.
3. Use humor and laugh at appropriate times during interactions with students to reduce tension, boredom, and other negative attitudes that threaten lessons.
4. Keep in mind young children have short attention spans and need multiple breaks in long lessons.
5. Use sincere praise, specific to what the student is doing.
6. Set short reasonable goals for students to reach, then celebrate their success when goals are met.

7. Personalize learning by pointing out good ideas suggested by students and show how you used them in the classroom.

Inside the Classroom, September 2

Today was a day of contrasts. The morning was wonderful, the afternoon was equally horrible. The four-star teacher that I felt aptly described my morning reading and writing lessons quickly dwindled into a charitable one-star rating at best. During the morning, I felt as though I were an experienced teacher fully planned and fully in control. I had fun with my children, gave them more freedom, and managed to teach many skills effectively. Teaching is great!

I had planned for the morning and afternoon sessions equally well and I am now pondering what caused the difference in teaching between the morning and afternoon sessions. I first looked to myself. Was I as well planned for the afternoon? Did my positive attitude become tarnished as the day progressed and it is my attitude that is the problem? This would be nice because it is easier to control my actions than those of the students. Next, I looked at the way I was teaching the math lesson. Were the lessons and activities for the afternoon lesson as worthy as the ones in the morning?

Many of my children could not follow even the simplest directions in the afternoon. I must teach them how to read and follow directions. I must help them determine whether their answers are reasonable. Is 4+9 really 7 or 10-3 really 13? I must teach them to check for reasonableness using basic algorithms with simple problems they can visualize and work in their head or with manipulatives as support. Some of my students had difficulty writing and reading the correct numerals for their answer. Some wrote five for an answer and told me it was six. When I asked them to put six counters on their desks, I saw counters ranging from four to ten. I know most can do the work, what is happening here?

Teacher-to-Teacher Commentary

The conflicts I experienced between the morning and afternoon lessons obviously have no single answer. Preparation is key. Math comes immediately after lunch. We had no lunch break because we always ate with our children so I had to set up the materials for the math lessons and review my notes after I led them back to the classroom. I was frustrated by the lack of time to prepare. My children must have sensed the change in my mood. When I relate the idea that emotions felt by one person transfer to another, I came to the conclusion that teachers' emotions are contagious. The students can feel the teacher's mood, even when the teacher tries to mask frustration and fatigue.

To keep the struggling students from holding back the rest of the class, they must receive small group instruction on basic numeracy skills. I must also plan activities to challenge my faster students such as expanded notation where they determine the place value of each number. For example, the digits 372 equal three-hundreds, seven tens, and two ones.

A Hundreds Chart is a wonderful tool (Figure 1) to help students develop number sense by seeking patterns within the arrangement of numbers, 1-100. The numbers are arranged on a grid in horizontal rows and vertical columns. Each row begins with numbers listed consecutively. As students study the numbers in rows, they will see that they grow *larger* by one. When they study numbers from the top of the columns, they will find that the values *increase* by ten and their value *decreases* by ten when reading numbers from the bottom to the top. From this, they can make up number stories to go with their observations.

My students could choose to sit on chairs in front of the Hundreds Chart I posted at their eye level and study it, looking for number patterns they could find and share with the class. In addition to counting by ones and 10s, they could find patterns related to place value, addition, and subtraction. One teacher told me that she wrote questions for students to pull from a box as they studied the hundreds chart. Questions such as, "What number has 10 more than 25?" In addition to the large class poster of the Hundreds Chart, I gave each student a copy of the same chart on a regular sheet of paper that they could use during directed lessons and put in their study folders to study during free time.

The following is a list of observations your K-6 students could make using a Hundreds Chart. Countless other ideas are available online.

Figure 1: Hundreds Chart

1	2	3	4	5	6	7	8	9	10
11	12	13	14	15	16	17	18	19	20
21	22	23	24	25	26	27	28	29	30
31	32	33	34	35	36	37	38	39	40
41	42	43	44	45	46	47	48	49	50
51	52	53	54	55	56	57	58	59	60
61	62	63	64	65	66	67	68	69	70
71	72	73	74	75	76	77	78	79	80
81	82	83	84	85	86	87	88	89	90
91	92	93	94	95	96	97	98	99	100

Joy and Heartbreak

Basic Mathematical Skills

1. Choose a number. Then observe that the number immediately to the *right* of the chosen number is one *greater* than the one you chose.
2. Choose a number. Then observe that the number immediately to the *left* of the chosen number is one *less* than the one you chose.
3. Choose a number. Then observe that the number just *below* the chosen number is 10 *greater* than the one you chose.
4. Choose a number. Then observe that the number you chose just *above* the first number is 10 *less* than the number you chose.
5. Observe that if you start with an odd number, every other number is an odd number and if you start with an even number every other number is an even number.

Advanced Mathematical Skills

1. To engage students in the fundamentals of skip counting, choose a number for students to skip count with. For instance, 3. Choose a starting number that is evenly divisible by three such as 21. Next count over to the *right* three columns. The number in that column will also be evenly divisible by three. Then skip to the *third* next column to the *right* and that third number will ALSO be evenly divisible by three.
2. Choose any other skip number. Say 7. Choose a starting number that is evenly divisible by 7, say 42. Find 42 on the chart and skip to the right to the seventh column. You will find 49 in that box. Forty-nine is ALSO evenly divisible by 7. Now skip to the seventh next column to the *right* and find 56, which is also evenly divisible by 7. And so forth. This

works for all numbers, if the starting point is evenly divisible by the skip-count number.

Inside the Classroom, September 3

We have already been in school 17 days. I had given myself a goal of establishing classroom behavior and routines during the first 10 days of school. We have made some good progress, but there is so far to go. Molding and changing children's behavior, I am learning, is a long-term process for some.

Teacher-to-Teacher Commentary

Dealing with student behavior is a serious part of teaching. I have found from talking with teachers during my frequent visits to schools and at national conferences, errant students are not just a rare occurrence foisted upon some unlucky teacher from time to time. Errant students are an expected and integral part of teaching. Behavioral management rules and routines must be planned, clearly communicated to the students, and practiced frequently. Above all, it is important to strive to establish a classroom climate that nurtures students' social and emotional well-being with the support of parents and guardians.

My friend and mentor, Ms. Miller, shared the letter she sends home to her parents each Monday. In her letter she describes what the class will be doing for the week, what the children are learning, homework assignments, study guides for upcoming tests, and other specific ways they can help their child. Before school even began, she communicated with parents and caregivers and invited them to visit the classroom. This is a great way to establish a relationship with the parents. I plan to use her idea next year to do more to involve the parents and caregivers.

Inside the Classroom, September 6

I see some promising progress in the children's ability to use phonemic awareness and phonics to combine isolated sounds and letters into actual words. The whole language people would frown on this isolated approach, but for low functioning students, I have embraced the research that has shown that students learning to read benefit most from direct instruction of isolated skills. Nevertheless, I want my children to apply these skills in a whole context experience as quickly as possible.

To promote learning of vocabulary, I started a 100 Words Club where students receive an award for reading 100 words from a word list written on a chart that I compiled. I began with word families such as cat, rat, hat in order to ensure that my students, with little effort, could use their phonemic awareness skills on rhyming words and experience success. I plan to use sight words that students will likely encounter when they read books independently. So far, my great idea has not caught on. I went over one of the lists with my class so my children could see that they can read lots of words. Though it was a slow start, I have had few volunteers successfully read 100 words. When this happened, I rang a bell, shook a pom-pom, and gave the children a colorful certificate to make a big deal over their accomplishment. I experienced absolute joy when some of my students gleefully pointed out words from the 100 Words chart in books they were reading. However, much to my dismay, many of the children who could read the words on the chart, did not recognize them when they encountered them in books.

Teacher-to-Teacher Commentary

The 100 Word Club I used came close to the beginning of the school year where I selected words that matched the basic skills students were learning. At the time, our class was decoding vowels and consonants and simple sight words. The word charts can also be used for blends, prefixes, suffixes, digraphs, diphthongs, and syllabication. In addition, you can list vocabulary from more advanced fiction and nonfiction books and units of study. It is important to say that the word charts helped students decode words and gave them a sense of accomplishment, something many lacked from their previous failures in school.

Although some of my children proudly showed me a word from the chart that they encountered in a book, too many of my children were unable to read them when they occurred within the context of a book. I erroneously assumed that once everyone could read the words on the chart, they would know them well enough to recognize them in context.

Decoding unlocks the pronunciation of words. Recognizing words in context is another skill that must be taught. I should have selected some of the words for the chart that also occurred in the books I read to them. I could have had my students raise their hand or make a signal when they heard words in a book that were also on the chart. During independent reading, students could have noted when they found words from the chart in books they were reading.

The use of words in a variety of contexts helped students learn to read them and comprehend their meaning. Choose nonfiction books on the same subject so students can hear or read the words in different contexts. Use these words while you are teaching. Reading books with similar vocabulary will reinforce and deepen the meaning of the words they are learning.

Inside the Classroom, September 9

I have been able to break away from the pitfall of giving stern commands and threatening my children. It was beginning to feel necessary and even comfortable to say, "If you do that one more time, you will miss recess." Or, "Keep your hands to yourself!!" Or, "Get back in line." Or, "Who told you that you could get out of your seat?" Some of the dictates sounded like excerpts from a boot camp for adults rather than a school for young children. I was beginning to think that this negative in-your-face communication is expected by the children and the only thing they would respond to. I could not believe it when I heard some of these words expressed in boot camp timbre come from my mouth. Sometimes it felt good and it always worked for a short-term gain. However, I learned that when I looked into my children's eyes before angrily addressing them, I softened my tone and the children began to respond. Days are not perfect, and too much time is spent on getting and holding their attention, but the children seem happier and I am less exhausted and have fewer feelings of personal and professional failure.

The children who get angry with each other and are the most trouble have a heart of gold when it comes to helping children with a problem. A little girl with cognitive and physical problems has been mainstreamed in our class for social events such as lunch, recess, and the time before school. I am so proud of my class because everyone is willing to make allowances for her erratic speech and movements and is patient and willing to help with any lunch room tasks. She is never without at least two friends vying to hold her hand.

The fact that if I fail, my students fail looms over all I do. This tremendous uncertainty is a fact of life. I cannot afford to dislike any child, lower my expectations, make excuses, or worse, give up by planning lessons that mollify the students and mark time until the end of school. My responsibility is too great to give up on my children.

Teacher-to-Teacher Commentary

The school culture is powerful and can suck you in. Day in and day out orders and threatening comments are barked at students at school. These harshly spoken comments and threats begin to seem normal. When everyone barks orders, yells, refuses to listen, threatens to paddle, and uses copious busy work as a punishment, their actions become the culture of the school. And thus, the cycle of negativity continues. Avoid these pitfalls. Stay true to your beliefs. Do not become a part of the students' dark world.

It was easy to fall into using harsh commands with the goal of stopping bad behavior. Yet these commands were temporary fixes at best. Furthermore, harshly-spoken words did not model the respect we are trying to teach our students. One reason negative commands have such fleeting effects is that they frequently become empty threats, just noise.

The effects of positive reinforcement, a desirable stimulus, are dependent on the time interval between the behavior and the reward. A promise made on Monday of an extra 15 minutes of recess on Friday is unlikely to change behavior of your students. The time horizon of the behavior and the promised rewards must match.

The conclusion here is that there are no easy fixes. We try positive reinforcement and, finally, punishment for bad behavior hoping something works.

Inside the Classroom, September 10

Tomorrow will mark the first month anniversary of returning to teaching in an elementary school. I have learned so much about the rules and regulations of this particular district and school as well as teaching itself. It has been an exhausting, humbling, and valuable experience.

Though it is a slow process, I am beginning to see some improvement in the writing of my children. If all children wrote on the same topic, I asked them what words they might want to use in their writing. I wrote their suggestions on the board and added a couple of my own. However, if I write too many words some students will simply copy them from the board.

I gave my children a laminated sheet of the 100 most frequently-used words for them to keep in their study folder at their desks. This has helped some of my better students. One child has actually memorized and can read all the words on the list. Tomorrow, I plan to give my children a different list, one that was given to the fourth and fifth-grade teachers at a faculty meeting. I plan to make a big deal about the fact this list was to be only for fourth and fifth-graders and that ours is the only first-grade class that has this list! I am hoping this will be an incentive for my children to increase their vocabulary. They are to keep this list in their study folders.

Teacher-to-Teacher Commentary

Students come to school with vastly different levels of vocabulary knowledge. In 1995 two researchers, Hart and Risley (1995), rocked the education world when they conducted a study on young children's language development to determine possible causes of the differences in the number of words they understood and spoke. These researchers noted that three-year old children in a preschool used vastly different numbers of words when they talked. To determine why there was such a large difference, they conducted a study on the number of words spoken to children at home in 42 families from three different economic levels. They found that on average, the number of words spoken to and with children varied widely according to the income levels of the families. Children from high level, professional families heard roughly 2,150 words per hour, children from working class families heard 1,250 words per hour, and children from welfare families heard 620 words per hour. An analysis of the types of words spoken to children revealed that children from high-income families heard more words of praise and encouragement than children from low-income homes. Commands such as, "Stop that." "Come here." "Be quiet." were used more frequently by parents living in low socio-economic conditions. The results of the studies showed no significant difference among gender, race, or ethnicity.

With such clear-cut results, the message to teachers is a strong one. Talk to your students!! Find ways to include new words in conversations, read books with high-level vocabulary aloud to your students, and seek a variety of other ways to expose your students to words. In your communication with parents, guardians, and caregivers emphasize the importance of talking to and with their children.

Walking home from a college football game I was behind a mother and young child. The child was talking and asking questions, but the mother was on her cell phone and did not respond. Since that time, I have informally observed the same issue between parent and child that leads me to believe that today's children, regardless of socio-economic levels have to compete with a cell phone to get the attention of a parent. It will be interesting to see whether the vocabulary level of those children suffer from the lack of interaction.

Inside the Classroom, September 13

Each morning before class begins, my children are to take two books from our classroom library to keep at their desk. When they are finished with their work, they can go to their study folders or read a book they took from the classroom library. The list of 4th and 5th grade vocabulary I gave them for their folders has been a big hit! I think they like to learn words intended for only 4th and 5th grade students.

Tomorrow we will decorate gingersnaps and vanilla wafers to make the face of a gingerbread boy. "The Gingerbread Boy" is one of the books I bought for the class and the children loved it! I plan to bring in gingerbread cookies for each child, chocolate frosting, colorful sprinkles, and plastic knives so they can decorate their own Gingerbread Boy. I hope my children can handle this. I get nervous trying anything unstructured and messy. However, it is worth the effort to have them make a prop they can use to retell the story.

I have been letting the children bring books home from our classroom library. Judging from the wrinkled and crumpled condition of the returned books, I think that they are being read. I plan to get books from garage sales to send home with the children. It is a good investment if the children are reading.

Teacher-to-Teacher Commentary

Given the devastating national post-pandemic test scores that showed a dramatic learning loss caused by school closures and remote instruction, reading test scores have dropped by four percent nationally (National Association of Educational Progress, 2022). Perhaps, it is worth trying the pay-to-read intervention to promote book reading by Roland Freyer (2011), a Harvard Economics professor. The results of his research produced interesting results. Through private donations, and possibly a grant, he worked with Dallas and Houston School Districts to improve reading scores. The intervention? Directly pay second-grade students $2.00 for each book they chose to read after taking a short test to confirm they read the book. Ninety percent of the students were Hispanic or Black, and 80 % were eligible for free or reduced lunch. The financial incentives for reading books went directly to the students. Results from the Dallas experiment showed that the increase in students' reading achievement was equivalent to more than two months of schooling (Jilani, 2022). In an interview with NewsNation by Jilani, Freyer said, "The irony is if you pay for high test scores, you get nothing. If you pay kids to read books or do math homework, you get high test scores."

Inside the Classroom, September 15

After school, I took some photos of the homes that surround the school. The neighborhood consists of small old homes, many are very run down with debris and broken-down cars in the front yards. There are a sizable number of single unit trailers surrounding the school and at least three graffiti-covered liquor stores within one to two blocks of the school. On Monday mornings several beer cans litter the school parking lot.

The juxtaposition of a pretty little girl with a bright red jumper and red bows in her hair sitting on the front porch of a ramshackle house has given me a fresh perspective of the backgrounds of my children. I know that most of my children live at the poverty level documented by the high percentage of students who qualify for free lunch. Yet, they all come to school so well dressed and groomed that I forget that many of my children come from less-than-optimal backgrounds. I must remember that they have their own unique set of ongoing experiences that may not match mine.

Teacher-to-Teacher Commentary

The culture in the neighborhood is reproduced in the classroom. The classroom is a microcosm of the local society into which walks a 22-year-old with a BA in Education from an entirely different culture with predetermined views of reality.

Many of our university students in the teacher education program said they knew they wanted to be teachers because they love children. As I did, they felt a pull toward children who are in need of a good education so they can rise above their environment. The hard work in the school of education was regarded by some as hurdles to get over, barriers to their dream of becoming a teacher and helping children. With love in their hearts, these students thought they were already equipped to move into their own classroom. However, they must learn that even though loving children is essential, it is not enough. They must also love learning in order to pass their knowledge on to their students. Love takes many forms: love of self, love of learning, love of others. In a successful classroom children respect the teacher, experience the joy of learning and its application to the real world, respect each other no matter the differences among them, and respect themselves as interested learners.

When thrown into the real world of teaching we have known too many teachers who became disillusioned and quit during the school year or did not come back after their first year of teaching.

Inside the Classroom, September 16

In the early afternoon, math was somewhat frustrating for both my children and me. My children do not have an intuitive feel for the processes involved in addition and subtraction. They do not understand why the sum is always the largest number in an addition problem or how to figure subtraction problems that are stated like this: "Three girls and two boys are on a swing. How many more girls are swinging than boys?" Answers ranged from three to five.

We acted out addition and subtraction through drama where three boys are standing in the front of the classroom and one left to sit at his desk. How many boys are still standing? We acted out several addition and subtraction problems using the children as props. I had one of the more advanced students write the problems on the board.

Mathematics, science, and social studies are taught after lunch. Unfortunately, the time teachers had to teach these subjects was taken up by bathroom time, afternoon recess, and dismissal. I noticed dismissal was the worst time-waster. Many teachers began at least 30 minutes early to get their students ready to go home. There were papers to pass out and students had to gather their belongings and pack their backpacks. Some teachers had students sweep the classroom, erase the black or white boards, and empty the trash. Once ready, the students waiting to be called were free to walk around and talk. Students did not all leave at once. Walkers and parent pickups were called first, early bus riders were called next followed by the late bus riders. Frequently there was a 20-minute gap between the early and late bus riders. Why am I telling you this? Because the varied times for dismissal made it difficult, but not impossible to find time to teach. However, I could use this time to give extra help to my struggling students who were still there. Or, a special mathematics, science, or social studies lesson for struggling or advanced students.

Teacher-to-Teacher Commentary

Though acting out addition and subtraction problems was one way to help students understand the concepts of more, less, and equal, it obviously was not enough to help them get a good grasp of them. Something was missing from this part of my lesson. The students were interested in the drama, but their attention to the concepts I wanted them to learn was short-lived.

I learned valuable strategies from a conference session by Anita Archer, a prolific author and dynamic teacher. She used signals to get students' attention. She demonstrated a way to get students' attention by putting both arms in the air to signify that something important was to begin and when she lowered her arms, all talking had to cease. She had us practice this several times by watching her signals. When her arms were up, we could talk. When her arms were down, we were to be quiet. Even as adults, we had to practice this several times. Undoubtedly, you can think of more signals to communicate desired behaviors. For example, the problem I had on the reasonableness of students' responses, could be addressed by a simple signal. Making up and explicitly teaching signals related to numeracy may equip you with strategies you can use to help your students overcome carelessness and inattention to detail. The use of signals may help your students gain a deeper understanding of the vocabulary and related concepts of mathematics and the actions they must take to arrive at the correct answer. Of course, signals can be used for any subject.

By wasting just ten minutes a day on dismissal over a 180-day school year, students miss out on 30 hours of instruction and learning. By reducing dismissal time, teachers have an opportunity to continue teaching their mathematics, science, or social studies lessons. They would also have the opportunity to work individually or in small groups with students on important skills. I focused on reading and math with my low performing students. After most of the students left, I shared a bag of pretzels with my children still waiting for their names to be called for the late bus while engaging them in shared-reading and math experiences.

Inside the Classroom, September 17

One at a time, my children have been using a miniature trampoline I bought at a garage sale as they answered basic math addition and subtraction problems. They jumped as they counted ordinal numbers such as first jump, second jump, third jump and so forth. They also skip counted by twos through tens. For the slower students, we began skip counting with fives and tens, the numbers most familiar to them. They jumped as they answered basic single digit addition and subtraction problems and followed my directives to jump more, fewer, and equal times as the number I gave them. A couple of the children were afraid, so I held their hand as they jumped.

My children had lots of experience in skip counting by twos through tens as they walked on the large numbers I had written on old file folders and secured with tape. When they got to the number 10, they repeated the process moving and counting backwards.

Teacher-to-Teacher Commentary

The idea of using a miniature trampoline was motivated by a math seminar given by the Orton Dyslexia Society. This seminar focused on strategies to teach dyslexic and non-dyslexic students to understand indispensable mathematics concepts through physical activity, recitation, and real-world problem solving.

I used the trampoline to give my students opportunities to move as they learned. In addition to math, science can be explored through experimentation with a focus on force and gravity. Even on a small trampoline children can learn through experimentation while they exercise and move. The idea of active learning on a trampoline made me think it would be very helpful to get a couple of stationary bicycles with a rack to hold books. My children could read and work out the wiggles all at the same time! Certainly, these bikes could be found at garage sales.

The sources for using trampolines and stationary bicycles that I checked focused on games and exercise, not academic learning. This is not surprising, however a miniature trampoline and stationary bicycle are such good ways to let restless students move as they learn. Please let me know if you think of more ways to engage students in learning while they work out the wiggles in your classroom.

Inside the Classroom, September 21

Yesterday, I reviewed the students' cumulative files to learn more about the ones who have been causing the most trouble. Upon my review, I learned something I had suspected about the children in my class. I have no students who did well in previous years. Their very brief academic history was dismal. One boy had all 'Fs' (Failing) for academics and 'Us' (Unacceptable) for behavior. Behavior was marked low for most of my children. Two of the children who had been promoted from kindergarten into my class had been recommended for retention but promoted because of the wishes of their parents. The other first-time first grade students had satisfactory reports, but not high. I will not use my children's prior performance as an excuse for poor academic performance, but it is disturbing, yet somewhat comforting, to know that the negative behavioral traits I had been working with came with the children.

I need to talk to the parents so we can work together to help their children succeed this year. I know that it is difficult for single parents who work to come to an after-school meeting. So, I'll have to be creative.

Teacher-to-Teacher Commentary

Retention and social promotion are two concepts that have been debated in education since the turn of the 20th century. Since then, like the ubiquitous pendulum, retention and social promotion, have been in and out of favor at every grade level. Now with the focus on a standards-based curriculum and a push for academic mastery of the standards for all students mandated by the 2001 No Child Left Behind Act and the 2015 Every Child Succeed Act, social promotion and retention are back in the news.

Twenty-nine states and Washington D.C. have now enacted a law that 3rd grade students must pass a reading test to be promoted to the 4th grade. Students in Mississippi who do not pass the exam after taking it twice are given an opportunity to go to summer school and be tutored by a reading specialist before retaking the exam. These laws are to combat the high school drop-out rate due in large part to a lack of reading proficiency identified in the 3rd grade. Mississippi's 2022 reading scores reported by the National Association of Education Progress, 2022 has shown that the learning gaps between poor (below basic) and good (proficient) readers have closed and the high school graduation rate is the highest ever at 88.4%.

In 2021, most states and Washington D.C. temporarily suspended retention of students due to Covid. Social promotion is the practice of promoting students with a poor academic record to the next grade regardless of their achievement. We don't want 15-year-olds in the 4th grade. We also don't want high school graduates who can't read. Which of those societal ills are we willing to accept? What can we do to help students lacking grade-level skills who have been promoted to the next grade? In a sense we have been chasing windmills by hotly debating the merits of only two interventions, retention and social promotion. We must consider developing and using interventions that prevent academic and behavior problems, rather than trying to patch things after they are broken.

Inside the Classroom, September 22

The first-grade students were tested today. To avoid pulling the teachers from their classrooms, the principal had the teaching assistants administer the Terra Nova Vocabulary and Reading Comprehension test batteries. My assistant was not trained to give reading tests, and I fear the results will not be reliable. After the tests were given, my assistant told me that our class was the lowest. This is a subjective judgment made on partial evidence. However, when I studied the test results of my class, even my good students, were reading at the lower instructional levels. I had no students who were capable of independent reading at grade level. I wanted a challenge, and I have it! Over half our class is made up of students who were unable to learn the basics in 1st grade last year. One of my hypotheses is that the behavior of many of these students prevents them from listening, following directions, and learning. The old, "He *could do well if only he applied himself," certainly applies here. We need to investigate why children, who naturally want to learn, are not applying enough effort to learn.*

I plan to read more often to my students, ask more comprehension questions, and find ways to help them develop their vocabulary. They are able to read the beginner books, but not the better literature. I had been reading "Charlie and the Chocolate Factory" to the students. This story is loaded with synonyms for the word big. As a class we made a chart headed by the word big *with spaces below where the children could write synonyms for big when they heard them in the story. This was a huge hit! My children became excited every time they heard a word they could add to the chart. I must do more of these types of activities.*

Teacher-to-Teacher Commentary

Though we were told to give the Terra Nova test for reading, spelling, and vocabulary, we were not given written instructions on how to give it. Today, information on specific standardized tests is easily available online. This link, https://www.tests.com/practice/TerraNova-Practice-Test, provides helpful information about the instructions. It has sample questions that include mathematics, science, and social studies, and tips to prepare students to take the test.

The results of the Terra Nova, no matter how questionable, was a wake-up call for me. Because they showed my students' areas of weakness in the beginning of the school year so, I still have time to help them. Now I know specific areas of weakness that my class and I can work on. The slower students needed help with basic skills with plenty of opportunities to succeed which will help break their belief that they can't be successful. The moderate and advanced students that showed fewer specific weaknesses will benefit from shoring up areas that are problems and expand their reading interests to more interesting fiction and nonfiction books. Thank goodness, we did not wait until the end of school to use formal assessment to test our students!

Inside the Classroom, September 23

Daily, my children filled a sheet of primary writing paper with letters, saying the sounds the letters represented as they wrote. Perhaps because these activities had become routine, they never appeared bored, there were few behavior problems, and they learned handwriting and phonics at the same time.

Honestly, it is obvious that I did not entirely embrace a constructivist classroom that matched what I had learned as a graduate student. In fact, more and more I moved to direct instruction. I knew what my students needed to learn and how to sequence the material so they stood the best chance of learning it. I kept the constructivist vision in mind so my students, many who were repeating first grade, would have every chance at learning.

I continued to teach phonics explicitly through repetition and drill, beginning with the vowels. My children marched around the room on letter tiles chanting the sounds for each of the vowels and wrote the letters in the air that represented the vowel sounds. We repeated this process for consonants, blends, and digraphs. They also loved to swat the letters hung on the wall with a fly swatter. I lined up my students in two lines and had one at a time run to the board to write the name of the letter that represented the sound I announced. For example, saying one of the three vowel sounds for /a/, the students would run to the board and write a lower or upper case "A."

A mathematics activity my students loved was, "Race the Clock." I adapted this activity from a commercial program. It involved the use of math worksheets with a large number of problems for the children who excelled in math and a shorter one for those who worked more slowly. After lunch and before our math lesson, I turned off the lights and held up a large clock to signal that Race the Clock was about to begin. When the big hand reached 12, I turned on the lights and the children began solving math problems for one minute. This was probably the most intense work my children did during the day. They loved it and groaned when I turned the lights back off, a signal they had to put down their pencils and stop solving math problems. Their goal was to see how many problems they could solve in one minute

Teacher-to-Teacher Commentary

Teaching can be divided into two large categories, direct instruction and constructivism. The defining difference between the two is the role of the teacher. The teacher either directs the learning (direct instruction) or steps aside and becomes a facilitator as students take control of their learning (constructivism). If you examine the words for each category, the terms direct instruction and constructivism almost define themselves. What category of teaching do you think Race the Clock fits into?

The self-driven competition during the Race the Clock activity required my students to race against time to see how many problems they could solve in one minute.

There is something wrong with this activity!! I am sure some of you have already spotted it. I realized I did not give my students immediate feedback on the number of problems they got right; their focus was solely on speed not accuracy. It would have been best if I had displayed the correct answers at the end of the Race the Clock race and have my students check their work to learn how many problems they got right. Or, I could have graded their work and returned it to them before the next Race the Clock activity so they could chart their progress on the number of problems they got right. This way the competition is between time and accuracy rather than time and writing speed. This focus on accuracy should motivate students to increase the number of *correctly* worked problems in one minute. The competition would be on math accuracy rather than speed. However, the kids love the race aspect so I need to build accuracy into the race.

Inside the Classroom, September 24

I created Special Centers for 30 minutes at the end of school. I planned them on the advice of a highly respected first-grade teacher who had whole-heartedly embraced the philosophy that underlies constructivism. During this time children loved working together on activities to explore, practice, clarify, and extend what they learned during my direct instruction lessons. I frequently changed the activities in the centers by adding educational games and puzzles. I always kept two of their favorite centers, Legos and a musical keyboard. My students' behavior was relatively good, though I did have to control behavior when some saw center time as a chance to socialize and play around. It helped to remind them of the ground rules for working in centers and letting them know what they could learn in each activity. I am convinced that behavior problems arose when students did not perceive their actions at the centers as learning.

Their favorite center by far was the School Center where children had access to markers, the white board, magnetic capital and lower-case letters, excess worksheets, and old unused workbooks. Of all that they could have done in the School Center, their favorite activity was to work on leftover worksheets, as many as they could do in 30 minutes! You could have knocked me over with a feather, I was so surprised! What was the draw to worksheets? Perhaps because they were familiar to the students and they experienced a sense of accomplishment as they completed them. The number of worksheets they completed was a visible product of their effort. I took them home and put a star next to the answers they marked correctly and offered a lot of written praise. The written praise, intended as a reward for their successful hard work, also served to further my children's reading skills. I saw them sounding out words I had written or asking other students about the meaning of my words.

Teacher-to-Teacher Commentary

Direct instruction is often confused with instruction from the more factory-like Dame schools or with tutoring from strict schoolmasters. The stereotype of these early 19th century schools conjures up thoughts of rote and joyless learning. At the time, instruction through teacher-directed lessons did not necessarily follow the essential stages of direct instruction models developed during the mid-20th century. Newer concepts of direct instruction are based on the work of Siegfried Engelmann who sought to improve the language skills of children who came from low-income families, were deaf, or autistic.

Madeline Hunter's 1982 direct instruction model, based on Engelmann's scripted learning approach is still used today. She defined teaching as, "A constant stream of professional decisions made before, during, and after interaction with the student."

To make informed decisions, teachers must have a solid command of content and pedagogical knowledge, a clear idea of the lesson's objectives, and break them down into small, sequenced steps. The five steps for direct instruction are:

    1. Anticipatory Set: Known as "baiting the hook." Teachers state objectives for each lesson, relate what is to be learned to students' prior knowledge and experiences, and use visuals or questions to entice them to anticipate what they will be learning.

    2. Procedures: Information is presented and acted upon through talk, questions, and other teaching techniques such as video clips, pictures, and directed hands-on exploration.

    3. Guided practice: Students work on learning a skill or concept while the teacher monitors and assists them. During this time, students construct new knowledge based on prior learning. This is also a time to answer questions and help students as needed.

    4. Independent practice: Based on assessment during guided practice, students work on their own or with limited help from the teacher. During this stage students can apply learning to new and more complex situations depending on their level of mastery.

5. Closure: A brief, yet very important part of the lesson when teachers restate what students learned, invite their students to think about the parts of the lesson they remembered, enjoyed, or experienced confusion. To avoid having students leave what they learned at the classroom door, have them look for evidence of what they have been learning on their way home or at home.

Constructivism is in harmony with the beliefs of Dewey and his famous statement, "Learn by doing." Constructivist teachers strive to keep the joy of natural learning alive by providing learning experiences that enable children to test and refine their hypotheses through continued explorations of their world. The following are three major stages of a constructivist lesson:

1. Opening: Open lessons with something to catch students' attention and connect to students' prior knowledge, experiences, or interests. They can include a challenging question, a discrepant event, an object, or a phenomenon to pique the students' curiosity and interest.

2. Body: The teacher creates a learning environment that is conducive to student-led actions. They can include, but are not limited to questioning, formulating hypotheses, engaging in first-hand experiences, researching information and collaborating with peers.

3. Closure: A time for students to reflect upon their learning and discoveries and ideas for further study and share them with others.

Even though the philosophies underlying the approaches of direct instruction and constructivism are different, there are many commonalities between them. Both focus on creating a learning environment that will draw interest to the upcoming lesson. Both relate the lesson to prior learning and student interests. Both enable students to engage in problem solving through hands-on activities and multisensory activities. Both have the lesson end with a closure activity. Those of you who feel buffeted between the two approaches, as I did, would benefit by understanding their commonalities and differences and matching them to the needs of your students. Knowing which type of instruction will be the most beneficial for your students is important.

Inside the Classroom, September 27

Lots of instructional time is lost during bathroom time. The boys have only one working sink and one cold drinking fountain. Put five boys around one working sink and there are problems. Put five boys in line at the drinking fountain, and you guessed it, more problems! We are working on taking turns. Soap and paper towels are usually gone and the students must get a bottle of soap from the classroom. Frequently children come back to class shaking their hands to air-dry them. A five-or-ten-minute bathroom break evolves into a major time waster that crowds out instructional and learning time.

To encourage the children to hurry back from the bathroom, I played a competitive game, Around the World, with the children who have returned. For this game, one student stands by the desk of another student and reads a word or answers a math question from a flash card I show them. The one who answers first gets to move "around the world." till he or she loses to another student and has to sit down in the winner's seat. The game continues until all children are back from the bathroom. My more advanced students appear to be more competitive. Surprisingly this works to their disadvantage. They get so nervous and shout out the first thing that comes to mind while the slower students often come up with the correct answer. This reminds me of the story of the "Tortoise and the Hare." I selected easier flash cards when low achieving children were challenged to give them a chance to stand and move "around the world." Most of my children loved this game! The ones who do not want to participate could sit in the classroom library and read.

Another thing we do while waiting for everyone to return from the bathroom is sing and dance to "Old McDonald Had a Farm." I have this song on tape, a rather rousing rendition. At first, we just stood in a circle and followed the directions of the song. Then I got the bright idea of writing out the words, "wife, "duck," turkey," and so forth. Now my children are reading words as they sing and play.

Teacher-to-Teacher Commentary

If you have not noticed by now, I get extremely irritated, a red-in the face kind of anger, when my time to teach my students has been taken from me. I sincerely hope you feel the same way!

To combat bathroom behaviors that intruded on instructional time and learning in the classroom, it was important to come up with learning tasks that interested the students more than their nefarious bathroom behaviors.

There were so many times that I witnessed valuable learning time disappear like sand in an hourglass. Based on findings from Kraft and Novicoff (2022), the students who need to spend the most time on learning tasks are in critical-needs schools where they receive almost 200 fewer hours of academic learning time. This amounts to missing five-and-one half weeks of school.

Since Covid, there have been talks about lengthening the school day or extending the number of weeks students should be in school to help students catch up on the learning they missed. A less dramatic approach would be to first look at the wasted learning time that goes on in the classroom. It is up to the individual teachers to replace wasted time with more academic learning time.

Inside the Classroom, September 28

During the morning, I noticed that one of my little girls was sitting and crying. Upon further study, she maintained an erect posture, not ever leaning back in her seat. When I asked what was wrong, she replied, "Nothing." During recess I asked her to stay inside with me. I lifted the back of her shirt and her lower back was covered in ugly red welts. Again, I asked and she finally told me that her mother had whipped her with a cord. Immediately, I took her to the principal. The principal called the Department of Health and Human Services and told me to leave the little girl with her in her office. Not more than an hour later I was called to the office to meet with the social worker who took pictures of her back and said she would contact the mother. At that point I was told to go back to my classroom. When the little girl returned to the classroom she was still tearful and continued to sit upright in her chair. The next day she came back to class and drew little hearts on notes to her mother. How terribly, terribly sad!

Teacher-to Teacher Commentary

The following is critically important to any one working with children. All states and U.S. territories have statutes for child abuse and neglect. According to the 2023 Mississippi Department of Child Protective Services all school personnel including teachers who work in public and private schools must report any known or suspected child abuse and neglect. This includes substance abuse, child trafficking, and sexual abuse. In Mississippi, people who report child abuse and neglect are immune from punishment because they are assumed to be "acting in good faith." Not to report suspected child abuse and neglect of any kind can result in punishment by fines up to $5,000 and/or imprisonment up to one year.

Chapter 3

October-November – Fall Has Arrived

Inside the Classroom, October 1

It is the end of the week and the beginning of a new month. I have begun to collect children's books, songs, poems, and art projects related to Halloween. Songs and poems are full of rich vocabulary that can be introduced and repeated in various ways through singing, movement, and the arts. I rummaged through a notebook I had saved from my earlier teaching years and found one of my favorite songs, "Three Little Witches." This little song is rich in vocabulary and has plenty of ways I can engage my children in movement as we sing. I plan to find some neat ideas on art activities my children could do. You can find different versions online.

Teacher-to-Teacher Commentary

I wish I had played around with the words in the *Three Little Witches* song to include math learning and help my students develop a sense of rhyme through phonemic awareness. Cardinal numbers such as one, two, three little witches, can be changed to ordinal numbers such as first, second, third little witches. You can extend the numbers of witches and create low-and-higher level mathematics problems for your students to sing and pantomime. When students change words to a song, they have an opportunity to follow, identify, or create new rhyme schemes.

Holidays celebrated around the world are exciting and something that all students have experienced one way or another. Because they share the excitement of the holidays and love to participate in music, dance, singing, movement, drama, and the visual arts, celebrations of any kind provide rich opportunities to involve students in learning through a variety of ways (Holmes, Moore, & Holmes 2022).

Many holidays originated in ancient times and their historical roots are frequently visible and easily recognized by today's students. Lessons about the times and places people lived will give students a new respect for the people who lived long before they were born. Geography around the world plays a huge factor on the origins of the holidays and today's celebrations that arose from religious and historical beliefs. One fascinating fact is that holiday celebrations around the world all have a major focus on light. Colors of light, candles, and light displays are prominent symbols of the holidays. Through history lessons on customs and origins of the holidays, teachers can capitalize on students' excitement while incorporating lessons on geography and other topics. Holiday customs can be integrated into the other areas of the curriculum. A distinct advantage of using holidays as a theme is that students have some prior knowledge and interest in learning.

Inside the Classroom, October 12

A full week has slipped by without writing in my journal. I am in the middle of assessing the children for report card grades for this quarter. Because so many of my children have failed the previous year, I do not want to give grades that they cannot maintain, yet, so far, many are doing exceptionally well. Trying to engage my children in active learning and because of the poor conditions of our copy machines, I have used very few worksheets. It seems unfair to use multiple choice tests on children who are not familiar with marking multiple choice answers on worksheets. "Test the way you teach" is a maxim I taught at the university. I decided to go with the authentic way of testing reading, by having the children read aloud to me. They read individual vocabulary words as well as passages from the stories in the basal readers. So far, my advanced and high middle students are doing very well. I will use a more quantified approach for spelling and math grades. We grade by assigning a numerical grade every nine weeks and a semester average at the end of two nine-week periods for reading, language, and math.

Today while I was testing individual students on their reading, I had the other students work in groups at the writing center, library center, reading games center, and the word wall. I only allowed three or four in a group at a time which worked very well.

Teacher-to-Teacher Commentary

The above entry suggests that we should not let the format of the test get in the way of assessment. That is, when we obey the "test the way you teach" dictum, it means that we should never spring upon our students a surprise method of assessment. If students have never used a multiple-choice fill-in-the-bubble test in the classroom, imagine the confusion for our young students when they stare at a worksheet or test that gives the following directions:

"Read each question carefully. Then fill in the bubble under the question that matches the correct answer."

If they have never seen a bubble multiple-choice questionnaire, what are their likely questions?

"What's a bubble?"

"How do we fill it in?"

"I tried, but I broke my pencil point trying to fill it in."

"Can I use just an /x/?"

This example of testing requires, at first, the students' knowledge of the testing format.
You want to test content knowledge, not test format knowledge. Be sure that the students are very familiar with the format and directions for taking the test.

Inside the Classroom, October 14

I have given my own individual reading tests this week to determine whether my students can read grade-level vocabulary. I first tested them on individual words and then had them read a short story that contained the same words. Some students read 46 out of 47 of the tested words while others could only read six or seven of the 47 individual words. I noticed that when the words appeared in context, my lowest readers were unable to read them, even if they could identify them when the words were presented individually. In addition, they were also able to memorize the words in predictable texts and predictable story patterns such as "Once upon a time," which they were able to use as clues for vocabulary recognition. Therefore, predictable books offered opportunities for independent, shared, or choral reading, even for the lowest students.

Teacher-to-Teacher Commentary

Predictable books such as *Brown Bear, Brown Bear What Do You See?* and *There Was an Old Lady Who Swallowed a Fly* were fun for my beginning readers. Through predictable books, children hear patterns of words that, when heard often enough, they memorize rather than read the individual words. Additionally, these books offer illustrations that support the meaning of the words. This first baby-step toward reading creates a positive climate upon which you can help your early readers build letter-sound relationships, vocabulary, and comprehension skills.

Johnston (2000) conducted research in three first grade classrooms to determine whether context helped or hindered word learning. She compared the number of words students learned using three reading treatments: isolated words in a word bank, a short sentence on a sentence strip, and sentences and paragraphs in a book. She found that first-grade students learned more new words when they were initially presented in isolation or brief sentences than they learned through passages in books. Why? Words written in context require students to understand the meaning of what they are reading rather than focusing on individual words. Higher performing students were able to follow the context and use it to help them unlock the meaning of unknown words. Johnston's research supports what I found to be true in my classroom. My lower readers were able to learn words in isolation but could not read them when they were embedded in sentences in their books. A word they could read in a list became a needle in a haystack when confronted by the same words when scattered throughout longer passages.

Walk into just about any elementary classroom and you will see a word wall. The article, *Should We Build a Word Wall or Not?* by Tim Shanahan (2024*)* will make you think! He describes the pros and cons of word walls and provides some good ideas for word walls that actually help students learn.

Common terms displayed on word walls help students learn important words they must know related to the content they are studying. For example, a mathematics word wall with simple and basic terms students will encounter during their lessons will help them understand the words when used in class, on seatwork, and on tests. The words ones, tens, estimate, add, subtract, more, less, equal, and reasonable answers would have helped students make sense of the terms when estimating the number of links that were in the chains DeShawna, a little girl who became a star, by draping chains around herself.

Inside the Classroom, October 15

I stayed late after school today and put up a few Halloween decorations that included a giant paper spider I found at a local store and yellow and black police tape that said, "Caution! Enter if you dare." I taped this across the doorway to the classroom. I think the children will be excited, and I am excited they will be encountering five words, each time they enter or leave the classroom. When it gets closer to Halloween, I plan to buy a large pumpkin for the students to explore physically and then write about their hands-on explorations. Many of my children cope with home situations that are so bad, that the simple fantasies of childhood are pushed aside by their complicated and brutal adult world. I hope that witches and moonbeams can add back some of the innocent joys of childhood.

Teacher-to-Teacher Commentary

The yellow and black police tape strung across the entrance to the classroom is a form of environmental print. Children see it every time they go in and out of the classroom. Environmental print consists of the letters and words young children see repeatedly on license plates, road signs, billboards, fast food restaurants, within stores, and their schools. Teachers in elementary classrooms can use environmental print to teach sound-symbol correspondence and sight word recognition in a meaningful context. It is an excellent way to expand students' vocabulary. Environmental print fits with the constructivist approach to reading where children are immersed in words through their environment.

Elementary teachers can continue this early word learning through direct teaching of sound-symbol correspondence by teaching students to sound out words in the classroom and use them in a sentence. Your students can find environmental print throughout their classroom, in school hallways, and the cafeteria. One kindergarten teacher made or bought a set of signs for block play such as "Yield," "Stop," "Exit," "Speed Limit," and so forth. A first-grade teacher made a class book of words from the fronts of cereal boxes as a cover. Another teacher has a Helping Hands Chart where jobs for students are listed on a pocket chart. The job names stay the same, but each week, the names of the students change. The names of the jobs are of high interest to the students and seen daily. Dinah Zike (2005) suggests having "On the Job Training" for the students for the jobs they are assigned to so they know what to do and how to do it.

Inside the Classroom, October 18

This afternoon's math lesson was a disaster! I had planned for the children to use red and blue Unifix Cubes to represent addition and subtraction problems. I was simply going to follow the teacher's manual which I thought did a good job of leading the children through the addition and subtraction processes by enabling them to visualize what happens when cubes of one color are added and subtracted from each other. What I did not notice was that my set of cubes has light and dark shades of blue unlike the ones required in the manual. My children were able to dig through the cubes to find red and blue cubes, but many came up with two different shades of blue. The ones who selected two shades of blue became confused. The entire 40-minute lesson was spent trying to help frustrated children use two distinctly different colored cubes so they could work the problems on the worksheet and answer my questions. In the chaos of this lesson, I learned more than my children. Always check the manipulatives and have them ready to use! I will try again tomorrow. After school my assistant and I sorted sets of dark blue and red cubes for each child that we will use tomorrow.

Teacher-to-Teacher Commentary

Little things that go wrong can destroy a lesson. In my case, a subtle difference in color destroyed a mathematics lesson. The lesson I learned is to look for any inconsistencies within the manipulatives you plan to use and get rid of them.

The Campbell University Wiggins Memorial Library (2022) website briefly addresses problems with manipulatives, but mostly focuses on a whole slew of excellent tips for teachers that will encourage them to use manipulatives. When teachers use manipulatives with specific learning objectives in mind, they provide a concrete way of helping students understand abstract concepts. The following are two of their tips:

1. Tell students what they will be learning through the manipulatives.
2. Give time for students to explore the manipulatives before using them in a lesson.

I remember attending workshops where manipulatives were placed on our table. Like our students, we all talked as we played around with them and had to be told to leave the manipulatives alone until we were directed to use them. One time was humorous, at least to us. We all had squeaky dog toys at our table and the inevitable happened, we were out of control squeaking our toys and laughing. If teachers, who are normally polite, break the rules, just imagine your students! By the way, the squeaky toys were to give us an opportunity to squeak them when we had questions or had ideas we wanted to express.

I have observed too many lessons where the teacher had manipulatives but did not let the students use them. Instead, the teacher demonstrated concepts using manipulatives while the students watched. An example from the Campbell University Wiggins Memorial Library (2022) relates this use of manipulatives to a teacher who eats a pomegranate in front of the class and tells the students how it tastes.

Inside the Classroom, October 20

At an afternoon district inservice seminar on RAISE, Reading, Assessment, Intervention, and Strategy Exploration, every teacher continued to have the same complaint about behavior. There is a sad feeling of frustration. They plan activities they are truly excited about, but unable to implement due to student behavior. We all shared ways we use to control our students, but the bottom line seems to be that nothing we have tried provides sustained improvement. Some of the ways for controlling behavior take a lot of classroom time, extra outside preparation to create and set up materials, and a tremendous amount of bookkeeping. The individual behaviors of each child should be documented and tracked with rewards and punishment meted out for good or bad behavior. The older teachers said that student behavior has changed dramatically. The respect for authority has dwindled, support from the home is lacking, and peer pressure encourages bad behavior. This communication with other teachers, though disheartening, was also somewhat comforting.

"We never know what happened to the students the night before they came to us." This powerful statement from a presenter at an earlier RAISE workshop reminded me of the reasons we cope with behavioral problems at school. It is highly possible that the students' lives are in turmoil, yet we just see the familiar faces with little knowledge of their family problems. I must keep this in mind when I become frustrated by the behavior of my students.

Just this morning the children kept up a steady undertone during the lessons, with the usual three interrupting by talking out and knocking on their desks. This was especially disappointing because I was truly excited about the lesson I had planned that had lots of active student involvement. However, teaching and learning were difficult because my students abused the active part of the activities.

After lunch, a parent came unannounced to my door during a lesson and asked to see her son. As soon as he appeared, she began a loud angry rant, "You'd better be good or your father will burn you up good, and I will also burn you up if you are bad!" Knowing this, his behavior would have to be really bad such as threatening or harming other children, before I send a note home.

Teacher-to-Teacher Commentary

Current wisdom suggests that teachers should focus on helping students develop positive behavioral dispositions during the first two or three weeks of school. When students practice, learn, and demonstrate the desired behaviors, the speed of academic learning will increase, making this initial investment of time pay off. This is sound advice for any teacher, and did help me reduce the misbehaviors in my class. However, like many theories, it does not apply equally to all students. I found that with my more difficult students I had to invest more time helping them develop positive dispositions, far beyond the magical two to three weeks. I learned that it was critical to plan and teach routines and dispositions as thoroughly as I planned for academic learning. This was not always easy. I found that desired behaviors must be broken down into small steps and communicated and practiced frequently as often as needed. This certainly beats the alternative, "SIT DOWN AND DO YOUR WORK!" that produces neither lasting academic learning nor improved behavior.

Teachers who focus exclusively on academics, getting through their lesson plans, *no matter what,* are doomed to reactionary discipline practices that slow down learning and leave some students out of the learning loop altogether.

I thought I had tried everything, except corporal punishment which I will never use. Upon reflection, the following are some things I could have tried that may have resulted in longer lasting effects:

1. Have students help to set rules for behavior and consequences.

2. Go over the rules and ask students why we have them.

3. Describe and show examples of bad behavior and ask students why they think the bad behavior happened and how they could fix it.

4. Ask whether bad behavior happened because of where they were, who they were with, how they felt, or what they wanted.

5. Let them discuss how to stop the bad behavior for each of the issues.

These steps could be followed by a writing lesson where students individually, in pairs, or small groups write one or two rules they plan to follow and post them around the classroom.

Good and Brophy (2003) studied the actions of teachers to learn how they coped with behavior with low-achieving students. He found that the effective teachers were realistic, yet positive. They spoke to their students in specific honest terms and conveyed positive expectations. They did not rush to tell students the answers, rather they focused on student learning. Ineffective teachers spoke in platitudes and generalities. They focused more on the end product rather the steps to learning.

Some fun books that can be used with younger students about talking in class are *Lacey Walker, Nonstop Talker,* and *Decibella and Her 6 Inch Voice.*

Inside the Classroom, October 21

Today was a day-long RAISE workshop and we all had substitute teachers. I have come to look forward to the workshops because I learn new things I can try in my class and, I get to talk to adults! However, we were all offended by the haughty attitude of one of the presenters when she boasted that she never had a discipline problem in her class. None of the teachers I knew believed her. We were too polite to laugh, but many of us had to work to control ourselves. The presenter claimed that she never had discipline problems because she involved her students in various types of movement through the arts.

I will try to include more of the arts in my classroom, but I will make sure they have a purpose. Despite the boastful remarks of the presenter, she shared many excellent ideas on ways to involve our students in kinesthetic and tactile art activities. The following are some that I think will be enjoyable ways to help my students learn:

1. Write the 300 words that comprise 65% of English written text on three medium size beach balls so they can be divided among three groups of students. Divide the students into groups. One student throws the ball to another student to catch. Students who catch the ball are to read the word under one of their thumbs before throwing it to another student.

2. Have students act out parts of a story to show comprehension and use of vocabulary.

3. Have students make up words and sing parts of a story.

Teacher-to-Teacher Commentary

Arts integration is important for many reasons. Students learn creative problem solving and critical thinking that can be used in any content area. Through the arts: visual, music, drama, sculpting, and media, students can take an abstract idea and represent it in a concrete way. Motor skills, social skills, and language skills can all be developed.

For movement, choose words to teach from the blog by Cox (2023) on the 300 most Common English words for the ball throwing activity. Movement for this activity can be for brief bursts of time, or longer periods of time to give students of all ages an opportunity to read and focus on the meaning of the words. In addition to learning vocabulary essential for reading, writing, speaking, and listening, students are developing physical eye-hand coordination necessary when throwing or catching a ball.

Act out parts of a story and make up words to sing to integrate movement and speech with learning.

By keeping the arts in mind during planning, you will certainly come up with many great ideas to pep up your lessons. Perhaps, like the RAISE presenter you can say good-bye to restless students when you integrate art.

Inside the Classroom, October 22

When I returned to my class the day after the workshop, bits and pieces of horror stories came out about the way my children acted for the substitute. For starters, De'Andre and Julious were sent to spend the day in the vice principal's office. Two of my girls were caught cheating on their spelling test and the children told the substitute they could go to the bathroom any time they wanted.

My children told me that the substitute was MEAN! Amongst other things, she used the fly swatters I have hanging behind my desk to swat the children's legs! The swatters were to be used by the children to swat letters, words, or answers to math problems, not as a switch to hurt them. All day long, my children came up and hugged me; one little boy said that he and some of the other boys cried because they missed me. Julious, one of my biggest behavioral problems, called me a "sweet teacher." My mentor, Ms. Miller, who also attended the workshop said that her substitute quit at lunch time because he could not control the class.

Teacher-to-Teacher Commentary

Stories about substitute teachers are legendary. Anyone who has had a substitute teacher or who has been a substitute teacher has stories to tell. Because they are not the "real" teacher, students feel free to take advantage of a newcomer. When I substituted in a high school, the students all changed their names. When I caught on, I renamed them using numbers, "Your name is One, your name is Two, and so forth. With a little humor I got through the day and was able to teach the lesson plans left for me.

Substitute teachers never know what they are going to face when they enter the classroom. Classroom teachers who had to miss a day unexpectedly may not have left any notes or plans. Others leave a full complement of materials and clearly written lesson plans. Each school has a different school climate resulting in differences in classroom behavior. The substitute is at a disadvantage by not knowing the students and not knowing the school environment.

Every state in the United States and Washington D.C. has different criteria for becoming a substitute teacher. Most require some education beyond high school such as a two-year degree from a college or university. Others require training sessions, while others only require a person be 18 years old with a high school or GED education. Many states issue substitute permits and all now require a criminal background check.

Inside the Classroom, October 28

This morning, I brought in a large pumpkin to scoop out later that day. I told the students they would be writing in their journals for 15 minutes about what they thought the pumpkin would look, feel, and smell like once I cut it open. We discussed possible ideas. To help them, I wrote some of the common words they might want to use on the board and we practiced reading them.

This afternoon, after I cut into our class pumpkin and the children got their hands in the middle of the squishy goop, I had them take out their journals to write about what they saw, smelled, and felt. I was afraid the children would be reluctant to write after such an active and fun experience, so I said that this time we would only write for five minutes.

Many children groaned and expressed disappointment that they would not be writing longer!! You could have knocked me over with a feather. I never expected the children wanted to write, but I was wrong. During this time, my assistant and I sat at our desks and wrote with the children for a full 20 minutes. After the writing period was over, I asked which children wanted to read their composition to the class and I had many takers. My assistant and I also read ours to the class. I think it is helpful for students to hear writing from more sophisticated writers that show that writing is used to express ideas through descriptive words and to stay true to the topic. It was a good way to model writing and set a high standard for the children to follow.

Teacher-to-Teacher Commentary

Writing words on the board that students think they might use in their writing came from an idea I learned at reading workshop. The presenter held up a book to show the cover and had us tell words we thought we would hear in the story. She wrote these words on the board and went over them before and after she read the book to us. I was so impressed with this idea that I used this same idea for reading and writing in my first-grade class.

This early in the semester, I focused on the main idea of writing which is to express ideas on paper. I did not focus on grammar and spelling; this will come later. Because reading and writing support each other, I wanted my students to be involved with words. I chose a high-interest topic, pumpkins, and let them become familiar with the sensory characteristics and relevant vocabulary before they wrote. This gave my students plenty of background information and words to use in their writing.

My students were involved in the first two steps of the writing process, Prewriting and Drafting. The prewriting experience was a hands-on sensory involvement with the pumpkin that gave them knowledge and vocabulary through exploration and observation. They would use these experiences to write their draft on the facts they had gathered. The other three steps of the writing process, Revision, Editing, and Publishing will eventually follow.

A great opportunity would be for students to write fiction where they wrote a draft of a story based on their pumpkin experiences. Writing fiction opens the door for writing stories about things that interest the students. They can use their imagination. Through fiction writing, students will learn to identify and describe the main character and the setting before delving into the plot. Later, students can learn how to use quotation marks for dialogue and ways to introduce a problem the main character has encountered.

Inside the Classroom, October 29

Today at the 1:00 recess, Michaela, with a tear-stained face, came up to me and said that Julious was trying to "rake" her. Poor little thing, I kept asking, "He tried to rake you? What do you mean?" I had no idea that she had tried to tell me something so serious. What she meant was "rape." I was told that Jaden held her arms and Julious made obscene gestures and touched her on her bottom. My boys, still children in my eyes, are very physically precocious and sexually aware. I filed an official report in the office on the boys who had tried to "rake" Michaela, but I do not expect it to do much good. Julious is already in trouble for bullying Dwayne, a small, sweet child, and other children as they walk home. What a shame! I shudder when I look to the future for my children, and most are not yet ten years old. Meanwhile, I must keep a much closer eye on the older boys in my class knowing that they are not the innocent young children I once believed.

On a much happier note, our Halloween party was a huge success. I brought in cookies, brownies, and put together a delicious ice cream punch made from orange juice and vanilla ice cream. I brought in two types of frosting, cookies and cream and chocolate, that the children could smear on their cookies and brownies to their heart's content. Though I did not ask the parents for food, some of my children brought in chips and candy. My assistant and I put the leftover candy in little bags for the children to bring home.

Teacher-to-Teacher Commentary

It is important to check the policies of the school for sexual health education before planning lessons and talking with students and their parents. You should do extensive reading of reliable and developmentally appropriate health information for the age group of your students. Find out the health needs of your students and what is relevant to their lives so they are comfortable in discussing issues with you as an authority figure. If you are uncomfortable, seek the advice of the principal and other community health authorities.

The most immediate way to curtail, and hopefully avoid, sexual problems is to check areas of your classroom that you cannot easily see. In many of the K-2 classrooms I visited, teachers created comfortable places for their students to work and some even had lofts where children could go to read using flashlights. Until I experienced the sexual awareness of my first-grade class with a varying age range of 6 to 10, I was not aware of the precocious sexual behaviors of some of my students. I took immediate steps to change the environment in my class so I could see all areas easily and watched them more carefully at recess.

Another way students focus on sexual behavior is by passing suggestive notes or pornographic magazine pictures to each other while they appear to be working on seatwork. A trusted fifth-grade student said that during seatwork, students in her school passed erotic magazine photos to each other right under the teacher's nose and were never caught. Be alert!

Insider the Classroom, November 4

Ms. Miller, my friend and mentor, a fourth-grade teacher, and I went out to dinner. As usual, our talk immediately turned to behavior and discipline. A problem we all experience, and it's a big one, is that the students do not have self-control. An example is a little boy who was caught pinching another little boy and said, "My fingers just accidently pinched him. I didn't mean to!" How many times have I heard, "I didn't mean to ..."?

Between the three of us we found we had the same problems when our students do not or cannot use self-control. They lash out, take things, cuss, hit, talk, thump on their desks, and jump up and move around for no apparent reason. They also daydream and sleep. When they are not called upon in class they pout, make groaning noises, and become angry. We surmised that if students are not taught self-control at home there is no way students will magically exhibit it at school. It is up to us to help them learn self-control. We deplored the negative atmosphere at the school and agreed that our best chance to change students' behavior was to use positive reinforcement. Each positive behavior must be taught and carefully nurtured.

Teacher-to-Teacher Commentary

Positive reinforcement is a basic principle of Skinner's operant conditioning, which refers to the introduction of a desirable or pleasant stimulus such as a reward after a behavior. This desirable stimulus is intended to reinforce the behavior, making it more likely that the behavior will occur in the future (Skinner, 1963).

Clearly, positive reinforcement is preferable to punishment when contemplating the options you have to modify student behavior. Positive reinforcement may involve transactions as benign as awarding gold stars or high-fives. My students loved to get gold stars. Although they loved to earn trinkets and awards, the bad behaviors, for the most part, continued in varying degrees that prevented them from earning many trinkets and awards.

Skinner would probably say that the positive reinforcement rewards weren't sufficient to overcome the positive "vibes" that our students got from misbehaving. Those rewards were:

a. Prestige and status among their peers

b. Lack of embarrassment by the misbehaver when caught doing something wrong in the presence of peers.

Despite Skinner's argument that positive reinforcement can change behavior, it is clearly true that changes happen only if the reward is sufficient to overcome the prestige and status that comes with defying the teacher or other authority.

Inside the Classroom, November 5

We continue to have Special Centers in the afternoon during the last 30 minutes of the day where the children choose games and activities. At this point in the school year, behavioral issues have become less frequent during this time. It is one of my successes. All of the activities that my children do are educationally sound in an academic and physical development sense where they learn, collaborate, and develop their fine motor skills. Students can also choose this time to write in their journals and read books from our class library. This is a time I can shift control to the students and be available to facilitate learning.

Most of the lessons are directed by me. I pair students, a form of cooperative learning, but my class cannot yet handle the freedom of larger groups. Even pairing can be difficult. Some of the children groan when I pair them with someone they do not like and refuse to participate. Once in a while I have a single white child enrolled in my class. When this happens, no one wants to sit with him. Statements such as "I won't sit with no white boy" are beyond hurtful. The damage is done. Nothing I can say or do can make up for the hurt felt by the child rejected by one of his classmates. I did not expect this attitude, and next time I will pair my little "white boy" with someone I think will be more receptive. It is curious, that my children accepted Betty, a white child with cerebral palsy who just began to attend our class daily for an hour for social interaction. This indicates to me that for the most part, my students have a big heart when it comes to helping others.

My assistant, Ms. Cook, is unable to control the class. She yells and threatens the children the entire time she is in charge. She treats them as major nuisances, showing them no respect and certainly no affection. Some examples of her classroom management techniques are, "Close your big mouths up! Shut up or I'm goin' to whoop you. I'm goin' to tell your mother and you will be in big trouble." In the cafeteria, on the rare occasion our assistants are required to sit with us, my assistant with her head bent over her lunch said, "Don't talk to me. I've had enough of you." Put food in your mouths and shut up." The look of hatred and the venomous voice clearly showed that she meant every word.

Actually, this hostile attitude toward the children is pervasive throughout the school. I heard one teacher say, "One of my students doesn't have a birth certificate. Without a birth certificate he can't be in school. I'm going to kick him out!"

I approached the principal and asked that my assistant be removed from my classroom. I was surprised when she allowed this. I have met up with many good and dedicated assistants during my visits to schools when I worked at the university. The one assigned to me is an exception.

Teacher-to-Teacher Commentary

The Law of Unintended Consequences is profound. Who would have thought that my attempts to incorporate some cooperative learning would end in hurtful racial expressions?

If you want respect from students, whether you are the teacher, teacher assistant, principal, or any school staff, you must show respect to the students.

Teachers should strive to have a positive classroom environment where students feel safe and respected despite their differences. Cooperative learning is one way to teach students respect for each other and their ideas. Cooperative learning is a practice based on the theory that children can learn from their peers what they had difficulty learning from an adult. Most of the time the groups should be no larger than four students. Though each student has clearly defined duties within the group, they also have a larger loyalty to work with their group to achieve the learning goals. Small groups can be divided into mixed skill groups where high achieving students help lower achieving students. The high achieving students benefit from teaching what they know, and the lower achieving students learn through a review of the material presented differently by their peers (Foster, 2020).

There are several ways to include cooperative learning in your classroom (Johnson and Johnson, 2018) and (Slavin, 1985). These researchers found that both high and low achievers benefit from cooperative learning. However, reports of other studies are ambiguous about the effects of cooperative learning on high and low achievers. Consider a small study conducted by King (1993), who found that in small-group cooperative learning the high achieving students assumed dominant roles whereas the lower achieving students were more passive.

During planning for cooperative learning, the teachers' work is behind the scenes where they devote time to planning learning goals, providing materials when necessary, and selecting cooperative groups. During the cooperative learning sessions, teachers are facilitators while students take charge of their own learning..

As for my teaching assistant, the comments in this and other journal entries stand. Ms. Cook was verbally abusive, yet the students eagerly sought her approval when they showed her their work. Even today, it hurts to reread the entries about the comments she made to my children, and the worst is yet to come.

Inside the Classroom, November 6

Ms. Cook, who has not yet been removed from my room, worked with a little girl, Olivia, who just joined our class and had never been in school. Why she was placed in first grade, is anyone's guess. At this point she cannot recognize or write her own name. This morning, I expressed concern to my principal that Olivia, who was far behind the children in my class, did not know any of the basic skills for reading and mathematics and was not doing well even with the full attention of my assistant. I suggested she be considered for kindergarten. That afternoon, with no consultation or warning, my principal stormed into my room, lifted Olivia, desk and all, and took her out of my classroom and moved her into the first-grade classroom across the hall. She stayed in that classroom for a little over a day before she was moved to a preschool developmentally delayed class. I was told that she is enjoying her new class because she gets to play in all the centers.

Teacher-to-Teacher Commentary

I hope Olivia gets appropriate screening. When there is a question of readiness, there are screening resources available for vision, speech, hearing, communication, and motor development that should be used before making decisions on placement.

Parents, guardians, and caregivers play a major role in helping their children succeed in school. The initial knowledge and skills their children learn long before they enter childcare centers and school are learned at home. Behavioral traits that include manners, self-regulation, and respect, required in school, begin early. Just speaking to children using a variety of words helps their vocabulary growth. Reading to children helps them learn to enjoy books as they associate books to fun or comfort. They also begin to build a foundation for learning to read by introducing them to prereading skills like the printed words, speech sounds represented by the letters, and ways to hold and look at books.

Exploring the natural world outside stimulates children's curiosity and introduces them to science in a fun way. Counting, sorting, and grouping objects are emergent mathematics skills children can learn before beginning school. These are all ways parents can give their children a strong start in school and aid their performance as they progress through the grades.

The knowledge and interest of the content areas that began early in the home, are further developed in childcare centers and then in schools. Today, the enrollment in childcare centers has more than doubled in the interval of 1970-2021 (Duffin, 2023).

At a Mississippi Department of Education workshop on the issue of parental involvement, the presenters suggested a novel way to attract parents to back-to-school nights, meetings, and other functions. They suggested we advertise that we will be giving out door prizes and small gifts to everyone who attends. Stores that sell everything for one dollar have a wealth of materials and inexpensive packets of items that can be broken into multiple gifts. Many of the large chain stores run deep discounts on seasonal items. Work with local grocery stores and farmers' markets for food items to wrap with a bow to give as door prizes. At the workshop, they had little gifts for us, and sure enough we loved them!

Inside the Classroom, November 8

My children are not good listeners and I must plan activities to promote this skill. I know that this skill can be taught and learned. Here are current examples of the levels of listening in my class: Before I even complete a question to the class, I have at least five children waving eager hands to answer. When I tell children to wait to hear the entire question before they raise their hands, some give me an answer that does not address the question. For example, if I ask, "What is the short vowel sound in the word pig?" The children will say the name of a consonant, "p" or "g." The more attentive ones will tell me the name of the vowel, not its sound. My children all know the vowel sounds; they just want to blurt out something, so they seize on related, but imprecise answers to my questions. When I asked for the spelling rule for doubling the "l" at the end of the word, many children read the word to me instead of stating the rule. Some children with their arms up and hands waving are completely spaced out, and when I call on them, their response is "Uh, what did you say?"

Today I brought in a large stuffed black and white dog I bought for $1.00 at a garage sale and sat him on a chair. I *explained that the dog would love to sit in the lap of anyone who is working hard, shows kindness to another student, or just needs a friend. I plan to let the students name the dog, and hope he becomes an important part of our class.*

Teacher-to-Teacher Commentary

The children who are not good listeners pay attention only when they are interested in the topic. They would much rather express their views on a subject than receive others' views. Left to their own devices, they interrupt frequently. They typically live in a stream-of-consciousness existence. Whatever they happen to be thinking at the time is the most important subject in the world and they want to blurt it out!

Does this sound familiar? Listening skills also plague adults who are not particularly interested in what is being said or cannot wait until it is their time to jump in and talk. We can learn a lesson from our own bad habits and apply it to the listening skills of our students. Did we overwhelm the students with too much information? Did we not make our question interesting enough for students to want to think about the answer? Was our question clearly stated to attract the response of students who do know the answers?

Modeling good listening habits in speaking to the children is a good first step. These steps must be taught and practiced over time. Do not be surprised if students are slow to imitate those habits. We know it's tiresome and dull to continue asking students to pay attention with sentences such as *"Listen to me!" "Keep your eyes on me!"* and *"What did I just say?"*

It helps to modulate your voice so that you don't sound flat and monotone and it also helps to use props, the more unusual the better, when giving directions or asking questions. Surprise the students with funny hats or even a conversation with a stuffed animal. Buddy, named by the children, has already sat with children who had been working quietly, working hard, or did something nice for someone else. In addition, I put Buddy in the laps of children I think need an extra friend. I was afraid my older boys would think my dog idea was corny, but they love it when Buddy comes to sit with them. All this is to say, be creative and do not give up!

In hindsight, I wish I had thought to talk to Buddy. I could have asked him questions such as what is 2 + 2 and have Buddy bark four times to give me the answer, or, I could have asked Buddy to repeat one of the steps in the directions I just gave. Something novel like this would have attracted, and perhaps, held my students' attention.

It definitely helps to model good listening skills when students talk through using eye contact, making comments other than "Mm-hmm," or "Uh-hu," and by asking further questions. Listening is learned, and therefore can be taught. Do not continually repeat what you say or students will blow off the first time you say it, because they know you will repeat it. This is something we all know, but bears repeating.

Inside the Classroom, November 9

This month we have been studying Thanksgiving. I bought large cardboard cutouts of Native Americans and Pilgrims and hot glued-them to the cinder blocks that form the walls of the classroom. I have lots of ideas for social studies lessons that I can integrate with reading, writing, and mathematics. Just last week, we compared the way we live to the way the Native Americans and Pilgrims lived. Through the Thanksgiving story we explored the character issues of hard work, helping others, sharing, and giving to others.

I checked out many books from the local library on Thanksgiving to supplement the few I bought. Each day, I plan to read and then discuss a Thanksgiving story. I hope to use interesting facts to interest and motivate students to further the learning of reading, writing, mathematics, and history.

Teacher-to-Teacher Commentary

From just this short journal entry, multiple connections between history and the other content areas, come to mind. Students can see the relationship between the historical first Thanksgiving and the joy of the harvest they shared with the Wampanoag Indians. They can explore how sharing a meal reinforces the necessity and beauty of getting along with others in spite of ethnic, cultural, and language differences. Students can make comparisons of the first Thanksgiving and the Thanksgiving they will soon experience. They can make mathematical calculations of time and distance for the Pilgrims' voyage from England to Cape Cod. Science can be taught by using various food sources, living things, how to grow and nourish them, and nutritional facts.

To achieve content learning and its application to an integrated unit, it would be helpful for teachers of individual content areas to work together on essential skills. It is worth the planning to provide a thematic unit where learning in one content area supports the learning in another.

Joy and Heartbreak

Inside the Classroom, November 10

I have passed a new rule that students cannot bring in money to the classroom. They have been bringing money to give to other children in order to be friends. This has been done mostly between boys and girls. However, once they give the money away, that child gives it to another, and then the initial owner of the money claims that the money was stolen. What a mess, one I certainly cannot resolve. Therefore, no money is to come to school. Today I confiscated two quarters and held them till the end of school before returning them to the child.

This occurred at a time when I had planned to set up a mathematics game using real coins: pennies, nickels, and dimes with two dice. Quarters would come later. Before the game, I put a pile of coins in the middle of the table. I reminded them that the coins were for the game only. No more than four students could play at a time. The game began with a roll of the dice. Students took turns tossing the dice and selected the coins they needed to equal the sum of the numbers on the dice. For example, if they rolled a "5" and a "1," they could take six pennies or a nickel and one penny. They used the money they collected to trade in as many of their coins as they could for fewer coins. When they accumulated enough pennies or nickels, they could trade them in for a nickel or a dime. The goal was to end up with the most money with the fewest coins. At the end of the game, one student was declared a winner.

I think the combination of money and dice appealed to my children. No one was to bring any of the money home. To show them I meant business, I said I would count the coins to make sure none of them were missing. So far, I have had no problems with my children taking the money.

My good mood over the math lesson was dashed later at a faculty meeting. The principal, Ms. Wrigley, said she was looking forward to reading the fifth-grade students' notebooks to check whether they had written the words of the day that had been announced each morning over the intercom. She warned the students that if their notebooks did not contain all the words, she would get out her paddle. She announced, "I broke my paddle on a little person, so I'll have to get me another one."

This was reminiscent of Ms. Wrigley's prior warnings about a word of the day all K-6 students must know. Each morning over the intercom she told us a word that our students must learn. Like her threats to paddle the fifth-grade students, she threatened to paddle any student she encountered in the hall who could not define the word of the day.

Teacher-to-Teacher Commentary

Money, even in small amounts, appears to be intoxicating to children. Quarters become valuable far beyond their face value. My children acted as though they were rich when they had a couple of quarters jangling in their pocket.

Because stealing was not an issue, I was able to involve students with real coins for lessons that began with sorting them into different denominations and counting by 1's, 5s, 10's, and later, 25's before advancing them into higher levels such as making change, estimating how much more money they needed to purchase a specific item, and so

Joy and Heartbreak

forth. Once students were familiar with the value of the coins, they were able to play the Money Game. I set up more than one place in the room where more students could play at one time.

The use of real money is certain to produce interest in the students, more so than fake coins, blue, red, and white chips or other tokens. However, you can use manipulatives that look like money to avoid having loose change in the classroom that can be lost or stolen. First, let students identify the fake coins and review their value. Then progress to the manipulation of coins such as counting before making analytic decisions such as, "Do you have enough money to purchase a candy bar that costs 89 cents?" "How would you make 95 cents out of nickels, dimes, and quarters?" There are hundreds of games and learning activities that can be used with coins as manipulatives. Just go to the web and search for "Using coins for math lessons" and you will have more ideas than you can use.

Because my children arrived at school at different times, I set out learning activities for them to do while they were waiting for class to start. Activities included the Money Game and Big Books roughly 22 x 16 inches on tables. My books were nonfiction. Even though the text may have been difficult to read, my children loved looking at the pictures, reading the captions under the pictures, and working together to read words from the text.

As for Ms. Wrigley, her announcement about the word of the day seems even harsher to me now than it did at the time when it was a daily occurrence. Imagine bragging about, "breaking her paddle on a little person…" It is hard to read and even harder to think that she actually said it.

Inside the Classroom, November 11

Today was filled with stories about what I consider to be appalling events at school. The most profound one, and the one that took a while to absorb, is Ms. Wrigley's statement about testing. The second-grade students at Hubert Jones Elementary School are to be used as a baseline to determine student progress. Ms. Wrigley said that she still did not know whether to tell the second-grade teachers to let their children do well on the standardized test. She said if they score well in the second grade, we will not be able to document substantial progress on future tests. Ms. Wrigley mused that perhaps we should have the students do a mediocre job! I don't know what she has in mind, not teach the children too much at the start of second grade or make the testing environment less than optimal. Excessive intercom interruptions would do it! Or somehow interfere with the test scores themselves. Did I hear the principal's message correctly?

Teacher-to-Teacher Commentary

The journal entry on testing was one of the most surprising ones I had written because it described the way administrators can interfere with test results to serve their own purposes. In this case, our principal, Ms. Wrigley wanted to show progress. Rather than working with teachers to increase learning that would benefit all students, Ms. Wrigley wanted our students to do poorly at the beginning of school and then somehow catch up by the end of the year.

The interference Ms. Wrigley voiced to her second-grade teachers may not be an isolated case. How many other principals, district superintendents, and higher officials seek to infringe on students' performance, as measured through standardized tests, to suit their goals? The intended purpose of the tests is to identify students, schools, and districts that need help. Today, the efficacy of standardized tests is being questioned. When constructed and used correctly, the tests should be an objective measure of what students have learned so steps can be taken to improve and further their learning.

Inside the Classroom, November 12

I try to send positive notes home on a regular basis. I bought some cute stationery and this evening I wrote general brief positive messages on several notes and signed them. I left a space for the child's name and a space to add a more personal touch. On days I do not have time to add a comment, with the exception of writing the child's name, the note is ready to go for deserving students.

The children love praise positive feedback and are eager to show off their work. Today the principal, Ms. Wrigley, came into our classroom and LaRhonda and Michaela showed her the letters they had written to me about misbehaving. Though the letters were written with invented spelling, the principal took time to read them which pleased the girls so much. I asked De'Andre to show her his writing. De'Andre was so proud that he showed her his entire journal! In his journal he had written a beautiful letter about how much he loved his mother, teacher, and God. With all she has to do, I was impressed that Ms. Wrigley took the time to come to my class and sit with my children while they read their writing to her.

Teacher-to-Teacher Commentary

Not only do students enjoy having positive notes from the teacher, but the parents do too. Positive notes to parents help build a relationship which in turn creates a team, student, parent, and teacher all working together.

Who doesn't love praise and positive feedback? It is always welcome, especially coming from an authority figure such as the teacher or the principal. Two aspects of praise that are important are these:

1. Praise should not be overdone. I observed a teacher, who was well meaning, but during the entire lesson, she loudly and elaborately praised each child multiple times with non-specific praise such as, "I am proud of you!" or "Way to go!" When everything is praised, the words become hackneyed and few listen or respond to the words.

2. Praise should be specific, not general. For instance, "You did a good job," is not specific enough. "You did a good job when you capitalized the letter at the beginning of each sentence," is specific. Not only does the praise feel good, but the student's capitalization process also is reinforced by the words of praise.

Inside the Classroom, November 18

We have been reading about Native Americans and the Pilgrims. I found a couple of fun short poems about Thanksgiving that I wrote on chart paper and posted along the wall for the children to read. Having charts around the room at the children's eye-level provides an excellent way to get them up and moving, something they want to do anyway. Meanwhile, they are doing what I want, reading! They do love reading the charts. Usually they work well in pairs, one is the teacher and one is the student. *The teacher, using a ruler as a pointer, underlines the lines of the poem as they read the words together. By working in pairs, the students help one another.*

Teacher-to-Teacher Commentary

As you know by now, my first-grade students are a lively bunch who have a need to move and to do work. I have used charts from the beginning of school thinking that printed words and numbers will be in front of them every time they walk by a chart or stand in line before leaving the class. Through the Thanksgiving holiday, students were introduced to new words related to the history of Thanksgiving and the food available to the Pilgrims and Native Americans. I wrote these words in short sentences on charts and posted them around the room to surround my children with words related to Thanksgiving. I did my best to write words and facts that would interest them.

Inside the Classroom, November 25

This is the day before Thanksgiving vacation. The children and I are excited about the holiday and the upcoming break. For a lesson on graphing, I asked my children to name their favorite Thanksgiving foods. Not surprisingly most said, turkey, cornbread, and pumpkin pie. I wrote these words on the board and asked the children to add more foods to this list. I chose four of the foods to head four columns on a large graph I had drawn on the board. The children were to raise their hands when their all-time favorite food was mentioned and I would count the hands and write a tally mark under their favorite food. As, I recorded the information, the children turned it into a contest. They glommed onto one choice, say "turkey," and cheered whenever another child said, "turkey." The graphs are certainly not an accurate representation of the children's actual preferences because they either answer "turkey" to get the applause and approval of turkey supporters or choose something that is lagging behind to show their own individuality. A study could be done to determine the desire for conformity or lack of conformity using simple math graphing activities.

Teacher-to-Teacher Commentary

Based on my journal entry, there were some things I should have planned to help the students understand the purpose of the graphing activity, what their role was, and basic ways to graph the information we collected from their responses. Once the information is displayed on a graph students can analyze the results.

I could also have done more to teach children how to analyze the data on their classmate's food choices. Other math questions could look like something like this: "How many more turkey choices than cornbread choices were there?" and "How many more tally marks would the cornbread choices need to equal the ones for the turkey?

A behavioral trait I should have taught my students before the activity was how to respect other people's opinions. Instead, I assumed that such a simple activity as raising their hands when their favorite food was mentioned was sufficient, but it was not! There were cheers and groans as students stated their preferences.

Chapter 4

December-January – Winter Holidays

Inside the Classroom, December 1

Since Thanksgiving the children and I have been in a festive mood. Decorations are up around the town and plastic Santas replaced plastic swimming pools in all the store windows. Signs of Christmas and holidays surround us and infuse us with the exciting feelings the season brings. The school choir, The Gleeful singers were practicing Christmas songs and we were getting ready to decorate the school hallways with artificial Christmas trees.

In what I now regard as typical, we were given an edict from the principal that every teacher will have a decorated Christmas tree outside the classroom door, or else! The "or else" hardly put us in the spirit of things, but it was effective. In a matter of a couple of days the halls were lined with Christmas trees transforming the school into something special. My tree was one of the last to go up and one of the smallest. I didn't realize that the tree I brought from home was so little until I set it up in the hallway. Not to worry, I thought, I'll just add lots of lights and let my children create decorations for it. To be sure, it would be the best decorated tree! To make up for its size, I bought some brightly colored satin ornaments for the children to decorate. But even with the added decorations, the tree looked small. I perched it on a stack of books and covered the entire base, books and all with a piece of red fabric. The effect was a well decorated little tree sitting on a lumpy base, fooling no one.

LaRhonda finally summed up what I suspect the rest of the class was feeling when she said, "Our tree is dumb." When I asked her why, she replied, "Because it is so little. Everyone else has big trees." For the rest of the week, every time LaRhonda became upset, she included our small dumb tree in her litany of complaints. For example, "Jordan is pushing me and our Christmas tree is dumb." Sometimes while standing in the hallway, I would overhear her muttering about our tree. I knew when I returned home over the weekend, I would purchase a large tree for my class. I want this to be a happy time for them.

Teacher-to-Teacher Commentary

Beware, there can be competition among classrooms, not by the teachers, but by the students. Walk down any corridor in an elementary school, and you will see works of children's art, cute posters, and decorated doors on all the classrooms. Remembering back to my own elementary school days, I do not remember whether I thought my classroom was better or worse than the ones around me. Therefore, it came as a surprise when some of my children complained that our Christmas tree was the smallest of all the trees.

The ordeal about our "dumb little Christmas tree" reminded me of other times students encountered group competition such as sports and relay races. Competition, necessary for survival in ancient times, meant life or death. Perhaps the spirit of competition is ingrained in the students today where it would be disappointing, not deadly, to lose. Had I been aware that my students would compare trees, not by their decorations, but by size I would have bought a larger tree for the hallway. The only good that I could think of that came from this "little tree" experience is that it groomed my students for the real world of competition. They do not always have to have the best of everything to enjoy it. However, this is one lesson I would have preferred not to teach my students in this way.

Inside the Classroom, December 6

Well, I bought a much larger tree for my children and I could hardly wait to show our new tree to the class. They were impressed. Because our little "dumb tree" had so many lights and fragile student-made decorations on it, it was hard to move. I left it in the hallway and put the large tree in our classroom where it could be easily seen from the hallway. The children made paper chains to decorate our new tree. It looked smothered with so much paper, but the children liked the effect. I also bought some wooden ornaments for them to paint. I noticed, too late, that the drawings on the ornaments were way too small for the fingers of my first-grade students. Colors smeared from one part of the picture to the other; it was impossible for them to stay within the lines.

I was very dismayed when I saw how the ornaments were turning out because I figured my students would not like their finished products. I brought out glitter hoping it could disguise some of the smeared paint. To my surprise the children were not critical of their work and loved their ornaments! They were so proud and eager to hang them on our big tree along with the paper chains. This tree has its own personality covered in decorations made with such pride by my children.

Teacher-to-Teacher Commentary

Thinking that the tree in our classroom, larger than most in the hallway, would make my children happy worked to an extent. However, a few never quite got over thinking that the tree that stood in the hallway was little and dumb. For them, the tree in the hallway that was easily seen by their friends and other students was better than a glimpse into the classroom where our overly decorated large tree stood proudly.

The arts, as basic as painting within commercially drawn lines, aids learning and development. The children were developing their fine motor skills. Even in the relatively small spaces, the children could plan ways they wanted to color their ornaments. An activity that I did not think of at the time that could have included more sophisticated art skills would be to give them large, perhaps pie-plate size cutouts of a circle to give them more space to draw and color their own pictures or designs. They could use the circle cutouts to represent their favorite Christmas song. They could have worked on them individually, as a small group, or with a partner. Taking this lesson a step further, they could have performed the song while showing their picture. I will try this next year.

Inside the Classroom, December 7

Painting wooden ornaments was such a success with my children, that I decided to try another ornament craft. I bought another set of large red satin ornaments, sequins and glitter. The children could decorate their ornaments any way they wanted. Because of the mess glitter makes, I set up a special place in the classroom for my children to make their ornaments. We ended up with some pretty wild ornaments, some with a glitter mixture that looked muddy brown. They seemed happy with their sparkly ornaments, but nothing has topped their pride of the wooden ones with the smudged pictures.

Teacher-to-Teacher Commentary

The holidays provide multiple ways to engage students in art projects that interest them. For one thing, my students had a real purpose for their art and loved the idea of being able to show it off to others. Since the October (RAISE) workshop, I have looked for ways to integrate the arts with reading, science, social studies, and mathematics. The five arts: Visual (drawing and painting), Music (listening, moving, singing), Drama (moving, performing), Sculpting (carving and shaping three-dimensional objects), and Media (imagery, motion, and change) all help students learn valuable skills that benefit learning across the curriculum.

To prepare students for the 21st century an emphasis on science, technology, engineering, and mathematics (STEM) became part of the educational standards in 2001. In 2006 the "A" for art was added creating STEAM. Not only do the arts play an important role in learning the other content areas, but they also help students learn to collaborate, imagine, and engage in creative expression. The National Core Art Standards (2023) address the primary areas of the art education: Creating/ Performing/Presenting/Producing, Responding, and Connecting. Each of these broad areas contain multiple ways that lead to student learning in and through the arts.

I looked for ways for my students to express themselves through the arts. It was too easy to limit their expression of learning to talking and pencil and paper activities. The National Core Arts Standards taught me to regard art as its own important subject that can be taught and learned. Through the arts, my students who struggled with traditional classroom assignments, had a visual and active way to represent what they were learning. Singing, moving to music, making up words to songs appealed to my students and enabled them to learn and show off their learning in ways that matched their interest and talents. Others found art materials such as clay to analyze, synthesize, and change the outcome they wanted. The five arts cut across cultures where students can use color and shapes to represent ideas important to them.

Inside the Classroom, December 8

Today was difficult. I think I lose my cool more readily if I am excited over an activity that ultimately fails, and that's what happened today. Previously, I had my children collect pinecones from the playground. Today was the day we were to go outside and spray them gold. I was excited because I knew the children would feel the thrill of their Midas touch when they sprayed and transformed their brown and somewhat ragged pinecones into gold. What I did not count on was the lure of the playground to the students. This morning when I took them outside, about half my class ran to the swings and slide while the other half was telling me what they were doing. I corralled my children from the playground and had them sit near me. They "lost the privilege" of spraying their pinecone gold. I was heartsick that all my children didn't have a chance to wield the can of paint. Instead, I had the well-behaved children spray extra pinecones so the children who had been in trouble would have something to decorate. After the pinecones dried, all my children got to decorate the tips of their gold pinecone with glitter and sequins. Glitter and sequins have become the mainstay of my Christmas art activities; anything looks good with enough glitter and sequins. I'm sure the children loved the messy part of this activity. Despite my best efforts to keep the glitter confined to the paper trays I provided, their chairs were covered in a fine layer of glitter. I had to laugh when I saw the children leave for home with glittering backsides.

Teacher-to-Teacher Commentary

Did you know you have to be a detective to avoid the chaos and disappointment I experienced? Wright (2015) looks at problem behaviors through the eyes of a detective. He found it effective to break down unanticipated behavioral problems into three steps:

1. Collect evidence of a problem behavior and analyze what you observed.

2. Analyze the conditions under which the behavior occurred and what triggered it.

3. Hypothesize reasons for the behavior and determine what steps you can do to prevent it.

In a different article, Wright, (2015) shows busy teachers how to write a task analysis on their goals for student behavior and learning. He even includes an example!

Wright's steps led me to think of the importance of visualization. Visualize all the things that could go wrong. It was my tendency to picture the things that could go right, in this case a beautifully painted pinecone the students could decorate as a gift. Though I planned ways to control behavior during spray-painting, I failed to visualize problems that could stand in the way of a successful activity. Yes, I brought out plenty of newspaper and cans of spray paint, I sent home notes advising that children wear old clothes that day, I had a collection of old shirts and disposable gloves for children to wear. I set up three painting stations so the children did not have to wait long to spray their pinecones. Unfortunately, I thought they would be so excited to spray their pinecones that I did not visualize the things that could have distracted them. Visualization can also be done by the students. I could have had them engage in visualization where they pictured staying away from the playground, how they would spray their pinecones, and the way they wanted to decorate them as a gift to take home.

Inside the Classroom, December 9

I found a website with Christmas tongue twisters. I copied three of them on large chart paper and posted them around the room. The students loved reading and trying to say them. I also made charts with the words to three of the children's favorite Christmas songs, "Frosty the Snowman," "Jingle Bells," and "Rudolph the Red Nosed Reindeer." We sang these songs often throughout the day. I used the words to teach and review sounds, spelling words, and vocabulary. Often, we just have fun. I have props for many of the songs that they love to use. The charts posted around the classroom provide a way for children to practice their reading at odd times of the day when they have free time. I keep one on a chart stand next to the area where they line up to leave the classroom for recess and lunch. I just love it when I hear two or three children singing a song they are reading from a chart.

Teacher-to-Teacher Commentary

If you are looking for a fun way to engage students with words that would promote reading, vocabulary, and phonological awareness, tongue twisters are for you! Just picture your students saying a tongue twister such as "Peter Piper Picked a Peck of Pickled Peppers," or a simpler one, "Toy Boat." Your students will have fun learning and saying tongue twisters while you are having fun seeing them so engaged and happy with your reading lesson. You can find tons of tongue twisters online and in books. The purpose for using tongue twisters can be as simple as a break from a reading lesson, or it can be an integral part of your reading lesson where you choose ones that emphasize specific beginning sounds, blends, digraphs, diphthongs, or breaking down words into syllables. Once students understand what makes some sentences or passages hard to repeat, have them try their hand at writing their own. The analysis of popular tongue twisters in preparation for writing provides a way to review words, their sounds, and the rhythmic cadence of the syllables within the words.

Inside the Classroom, December 10

The local newspaper was soliciting letters written to Santa. I wanted my children to participate knowing this was an excellent opportunity for them to write about something important to them for a real audience. They were excited when I mentioned it. I asked my assistant to help the children she was tutoring write letters to Santa for the paper. I told her to let them make up their own stories using invented spelling when needed. After she left, we began to write our letters. Using parts of the writing process, we brainstormed things we would say in our letters. I wrote key words on the board. The children all have laminated lists of Dolch's 100 most frequently used words in a study folder at their desks along with the lists of the 5th grade words I gave them a few weeks ago to consult. I felt I had done a good job preparing my students to write because they were eager to begin writing. When they were done, most wanted to read what they had written to the class. The results were predictable, with some children writing far more than others. Because of their high interest, overall, the quality of their writing was quite good.

When my assistant returned, I asked to see the letters her children had written so I could include them with the ones written by the rest of the class. She gave me a single letter and it was very well written. As it turns out, she wrote the letter and had her students copy it. This was such a wasted moment for my lowest readers to write their own letters. I mailed the letters my children had written to the newspaper. Now we will wait to see whether we are published.

Teacher-to-Teacher Commentary

To help students have a chance to be published in the local newspaper, I followed the five stages of the writing process: prewriting, drafting, revising, editing, and publishing, with the hope of having at least one of our letters

Joy and Heartbreak

published in the newspaper. The stages of the writing process enable you to break down a writing task into manageable steps that do not overwhelm your students. I was able to focus on each stage of writing rather than just telling my students to write a letter to Santa. Take time to involve your students in the stages:

> Prewriting: This stage provides the foundation of your students' writing. Don't rush this one! During prewriting, let students know the audience and purpose of their writing, have students brainstorm ideas of the things they want to include in their letters and plan what they want to say.
>
> Drafting: Once students have a clear idea of what they want to include in their letter they are ready to write a rough draft, sometimes called a sloppy copy. This is the student's first attempt to get their thoughts down on paper in a coherent way. Assure them they will have time to correct mistakes and change what they want to say.
>
> Revising: This is best done after a lapse of time, at least a day. Students engage in revising their work during the next day's writing lesson. They should look for spelling and grammatical errors, clarity, flow of their writing, and ways to make it more interesting to the reader.
>
> Editing: Not to be confused with revision, this is essentially a nitpicking time, a time for students to make final corrections for spelling, punctuation, sentence construction, and grammar along with any other nit they

find. Students would do well to wait a day before editing so they can view their work with fresh eyes. Reading their work aloud to themselves or to you is a good way your students can catch errors and think of changes they want to make.

Publishing: The culmination of writing which is ready to show to an audience. It is ideal to have varied audiences in addition to the teacher such as a parent night or another class. Be as creative as possible to find places within your community to display your students' work.

Though all the steps are eventually important, my first-grade students needed more time to engage in the prewriting and drafting stages. Revising was often difficult in part because of their labored handwriting. Have slower students or reluctant writers dictate their thoughts to you as you write them word for word. Read, or have your students read their thoughts out loud so they can hear and identify possible changes they would like to make.

Engaging your students in the stages of the writing process, though useful for all types of writing, will vary based on the age of your students, their previous writing experiences, and reasons for writing. The journal writing my students engaged in each morning was an outpouring of thoughts with no intended audience except for themselves, and, occasionally, the teacher. Younger students most likely will remain in the prewriting stage longer trying to gather their ideas and determine what they want to say. By being a supportive audience, you can give your students confidence and help them view themselves as writers.

Joy and Heartbreak

Inside the Classroom, December 14

My assistant, Ms. Cook, comes infrequently to our class. When she does come, the children greet her as though she were Oprah Winfrey. Her response, if she gives them one, is to make a hushing sound. Perhaps she doesn't want to interrupt their work, but I think I'm being charitable. It is sad because my children want to share with her the projects they have completed and the charts they can read, but she just goes about her business at her desk and leaves.

This morning Ms. Cook came in with Christmas presents and some Christmas cards. I felt a softening toward her; I was touched she would remember the children. However, my good feelings toward her were short-lived. With no regard for the reading lesson she had interrupted, she handed a large well wrapped gift to Jasmine, her favorite student. She gave two much smaller gifts to two other girls who apparently ranked second and third in her favor. The other girls received Christmas cards, and NOTHING for the boys; she stiffed the boys entirely. When she left, the interrupted lesson was the least of my worries. She had created envy and discontent among my girls and bewilderment among the boys. Some of my boys, interestingly the biggest and the toughest, were close to tears. Julious summed it up by saying, "I guess she doesn't like us."

I have puzzled over the children's positive response to Ms. Cook. She is rude and neglectful, yet my children appear to love her. Could it be that being Black and sharing their background has created an invincible bond? LaRhonda, the little girl whose mother died, has been the most desirous of Ms. Cook's attention. She clings to her, draws her pictures, and looks at her with such longing. Try as I might, I can't even begin to fill the void in LaRhonda's life, but I believe Ms. Cook could if she wanted to. Sadly, LaRhonda was one of the girls who did not receive a gift. At that very moment, LaRhonda knew she had been rejected by someone she adored. It broke my heart.

Teacher-to-Teacher Commentary

My assistant's blatant show of favoritism had a profound effect on the children who did not receive her blessing expressed by her distribution of gifts and cards. The saying, "Believe in me, and I will too" aptly describes the Pygmalion phenomenon based on a Greek artist who made a sculpture of a woman so beautiful that he fell in love with her, thus bringing her to life. My assistant created this phenomenon in reverse where before my very eyes, the lively faces of my children were extinguished by someone who did not love, or even like them. The students who had received no gifts or cards realized their self-worth. Had their expressions been sculpted, their sculptures would have shown the heartbreak and anguish of their greatly reduced self-worth. I had a difficult time after she left, trying to assure my students that they were all a very important part of the class.

Inside the Classroom, December 17

This morning, the last day of school before vacation, the principal kept the lights out in the hallway after classes began. With all the trees, our ordinary hallway was transformed into a glittering fairyland. After arming the children with books and other activities they could do at their desks, I took the children into the hall two at a time. I had them close their eyes and led them out of the classroom to see the magical effect of a hallway lit up by Christmas lights. I was not disappointed by their reaction. My children stood silently taking in the beauty and magic of the lights. Many stood for a long time before exclaiming how beautiful it was. Briefly, they had entered another world. The effect will stay with me for a long time and I hope it does the same for my children. They deserve beauty in their world.

The children brought in little gifts for me and my assistant, Ms. Cook. I am now in possession of an 8x10 portrait of Julious, one of my older boys who has tried my patience on numerous occasions. Now there is no chance I will ever forget him. My best Christmas gift came from LaRhonda, the little girl who is still struggling with the death of her mother. She gave Ms. Cook and me a stack of used Christmas cards. LaRhonda was so excited showing me each of the cards and exclaiming how pretty they were. She was so proud of her gift to me. LaRhonda's gift truly symbolizes the spirit of Christmas. I had wrapped books, miniature crystal garden kits, and wrote a card to give to each child.

By now the children have forgotten about the possibility of having their letters published in the newspaper. I've continued to check and have not seen them. Some of the teachers who live in the area said they would check the paper for me after school lets out for Christmas break. I am beginning to think our letters did not make it into the paper this year but there still is time to hope.

Some of the best advice I received while teaching this year came from my principal, Ms. Wrigley. As I was packing my car to go home for Christmas vacation she said, "When you are at school give all you have to your class. When you are at home, leave your classroom behind." I have an exciting Christmas break planned with my family. I'll do my best to follow her advice.

Teacher-to-Teacher Commentary

Though the magical effect of the lighted Christmas trees in a darkened hallway had a profound effect on my students, students can and should experience beauty in many other ways. You do not have to go to such extremes to create a beautiful setting for your students. The following are a few ways to include beauty in your planning:

1. Show the beauty in your students' hard work by creating flashy displays of their work. For example, to make displays personal, take pictures of your children holding a paper they did well or a noteworthy project to put on a colorful bulletin board. For one display I bought an inexpensive pack of children's sunglasses and removed the lenses so the children could wear them and pretend they were a movie or rock star. I took their pictures and hung them on the bulletin board with the heading, "Tiger Stars!!!" If you recall, at the beginning of the year, my students chose the name Tiger for our class.

2. Attach crepe paper streamers over the door students go through when entering the classroom related to the theme they will be studying. The beauty is not only in a colorful entrance, but in the curiosity, interest, and expectations experienced by the students.

3. Play music to accompany physical activities. Soft music can add a beautiful soothing sound or an energetic march or fast-paced appropriate popular music adds beauty through sound. Your students will respond even more if you

choose music familiar to them. I found and included their music after my students called the music I was playing, "my music." Music adds to the beauty of an activity because it is shared by everyone, enables physical expression, stirs the imagination, and is just plain fun!

4. A smile is beautiful. Laughter can be even more beautiful, all without saying a word. These simple traits show children a bright side of life, that unfortunately some rarely experience outside the classroom. The beauty of a smile or laughter is that it replaces negative emotions with pleasurable feelings, reduces stress, and can be contagious. Smiles and laughter can be directed at a particular child and the whole class. These actions must be genuine and be frequent.

5. Reading and showering your students with books with beautiful stories, poems, and illustrations can add beauty to your student's world. There are many books that are about beauty that can be found on the Internet. A site from Character Kid Lit lists books that inspire awe and wonder and contains descriptions of several books that include nonfiction, graphic novels, and fiction. The book, *When the Sky Glows*, is an example of a picture book that combines science and beauty. You may have your own favorite books that emphasize beauty. One of mine that I have loved over the years is *Beautiful Joe*. It is a story of the way beauty arose from an act of animal cruelty. The story is told through the eyes of the dog, Joe, who lived with the kind family who rescued him.

Inside the Classroom, January 3

We are in a new year, hopefully refreshed and ready for school to resume after a two-week break. My children seemed happy to be back and I had thought of a lot of plans for helping them learn. I was eager to see my children and find out what they had been doing during their school vacation. Fortunately, there were no sad tales of disappointment or family events that took place over the holidays.

Before the Christmas break, I worked out a cross-age reading plan with a kindergarten teacher. Today, my students chose a book to read to a kindergarten child and will practice reading it during the week. On Fridays they will sit on the floor with one or two kindergarten students and read their book to them. When they return to our classroom, I will write their good and bad experiences on chart paper and discuss them.

Teacher-to-Teacher Commentary

Going from a long break that provided freedom to sleep in and choose your own tasks to the return to your highly responsible job of planning and teaching a classroom full of students can be difficult. The same holds true for your students, even more so because they likely had fewer responsibilities at home. Therefore, put on your happy face and warmly welcome them as they return to class. If you have time, freshen your classroom with pictures of interest, different games and manipulatives, and display new books you bought or checked out from the library. In other words, brighten your classroom in a way that gives your students the feeling of a fresh start.

Undoubtably, some students may be anxious that they will not fit in with friends, others will be excited to return to school. Teachers can do a few things to make this transition easier. For example, provide breaks in the lessons where students can exercise, engage in shared conversation, laugh at an oddity such as a singing flower or singing fish (Remember those?) and a seasonable Mad Libs story. In addition, when you get down to the serious business of teaching your daily lessons, plan and emphasize the anticipatory set (the way you open your lesson) using visuals and sounds to create interest. This will enable you to recapture your students' attention and interest them in the upcoming lesson.

I plan to continue cross-age reading with the kindergarten students. The debriefing sessions. will provide real-world opportunities to address the things that worked and problems they encountered. Cross-age reading is also an opportunity for students to discuss basic reading skills such as comprehension strategies and fluency. I see possibilities for my students to use phonics and learn new vocabulary during their daily practice sessions. By writing their concerns and ideas on a chart, I will be able to teach and review important reading strategies proposed by my students in a meaningful way.

Inside the Classroom, January 7

I was always on the lookout for books that would tempt my students to read. In preparation for celebrating Martin Luther King's birthday, I went to the city library and brought in several books about his life. One little boy, the one who had been retained three times, carried around a book on Martin Luther King, almost lovingly, and read it every chance he had. He had tears in his eyes when he talked about his hero, Martin Luther King. Other popular books were Great Black Heroes and Five Brave Explorers.

Teacher-to-Teacher Commentary

Because almost all of the children I taught were Black, I was constantly looking for Black heroes they could look up to and emulate. Finding books was not difficult. Many books on Black heroes are available in libraries, bookstores, and online. They were the most popular books in our classroom library and remained popular for the rest of the school year. Because the celebration of Martin Luther King's birthday came in January, many of my children had built up their knowledge of sight words and used their decoding skills to read unfamiliar words in the books they chose to read. Looking back, I wish I had not waited so long to introduce and focus on Black heroes. My children would have benefited from their beliefs and accomplishments all year long, not just on days that led up to Black history month and Martin Luther King's birthday.

The following is a sample of quotations from famous Black people that can inspire your students, Black and white. I wish I had emphasized one famous person a week where we discussed his or her background and accomplishments, the meaning of the quote, and how it relates to positive behaviors including hard work and perseverance.

To Encourage Writing

Maya Dwayne, a proliferate writer of poems and books
"While one may encounter many defeats, one must not be defeated."

Frederick Douglas, a slave born in 1818 who wrote a best-selling autobiography
"Without a struggle there can be no progress."

To Encourage Positive Traits

Martin Luther King, Baptist minister and famous leader for civil rights through nonviolence
"Time is always right to do what is right."

Thomas Sowell, a prolific writer and commentator
"You cannot subsidize irresponsibility and expect people to become more responsible."
Ben Carson, presidential candidate and brain surgeon
"Success is determined not by whether you face obstacles, but by your reaction to them."
Jay-Z, rapper and businessman
"The genius thing that we did was, we didn't give up."
<u>To Overcome Struggles</u>
Colin Powell, Army officer and first Black Secretary of State
"A dream doesn't become a reality through magic; it takes sweat, determination, and hard work."
Oprah Winfrey, famous talk show host and author
"Don't put a ceiling on yourself."
Nelson Mandela, first South African president known for ending racial segregation
"We must use time wisely."
"It always seems impossible until it is done."
Shelby Steele, author and film maker
"Opportunity follows struggle. It follows effort. It follows hard work. It doesn't come before."

Inside the Classroom, January 10

In preparation for Martin Luther King's birthday, I have been reading Martin Luther King books to my children. These books were constantly in their hands. De'Andre continued to carry around his book on MLK saying that he wishes he had known him. My children really like having a Black hero to look up to. I emphasized that Martin Luther King prized education and worked hard to strive for his dream of equality and nonviolence. This led to some great discussions on how Martin Luther King would have acted in school.

My children were willing to read books at any level about Black heroes. I plan to bring in more books about Black sports figures, Black inventors, and other Black heroes.

Teacher-to-Teacher Commentary

Because the children I taught were mostly Black and I had seen their intense interest in Black heroes, namely Martin Luther King and Tiger Woods, I wanted to keep their interest high in the achievement of people they could relate to who overcame hardships by working hard to meet their goals. The way I found to interest my students in the hardships and successes of Black heroes was through books on Black heroes. I have named a few, but it would be best if you explored the books available to children online, in bookstores, and the public library. Three that I found are *Black Heroes of the American Revolution, Great Black Heroes,* and *Five Brilliant Scientists.*

Black History Month and Martin Luther King's birthday were great times to double down and help my children learn about and celebrate the contributions made by people with backgrounds and goals just like them. I wanted to use books with the pictures, quotes, messages, and stories behind each one of the Black heroes to keep them alive daily in my children's lives all year long. I wanted to help my children learn that working toward success did not begin as an adult, but rather it began as a young child, just like them.

I also wanted to emphasize the positive traits shown by Black heroes and contrast them with negative behaviors such as drug use, gangs, violence, crime, and neglect long after Martin Luther King's birthday and Black History month. Information from books on Black heroes would have helped me greatly to teach and discuss the problems they faced as children and the ways they overcame them. My goal was to have Black heroes become a stronger presence in my children's lives than people with negative influences they might encounter on the streets. Next year I will plan more ways to involve my students with people they look up to and make it a major part of my curriculum.

Inside the Classroom, January 17

Today is the holiday when we celebrate Martin Luther King's birthday! His actual birthday is January 15. We spent a lot of time talking about Martin Luther King and what he stood for. The night before, I hung up a banner in the front of my class with one of his quotes that said, "A man is not judged by what he wants to do. He is judged by what he does do." I wish I had thought to put a couple of balloons around Martin Luther King's quote to draw my students' attention to it and highlight his birthday. I was able to read it with my children frequently and discuss behaviors in school that would have made Martin Luther King proud.

Teacher-to-Teacher Commentary

You can capitalize on your students' interest in books and quotations from Black heroes by focusing on vocabulary. Words within the quotes you posted will not leap off the paper without some help from you. Directly teach unusual or unknown words. Before asking students to read a new quotation, check for prefixes and suffixes that the words may contain and teach or review them with your class.

Think of ways to teach the meaning of the words visually through commercial or student drawn illustrations. Model curiosity about the meaning of the words you don't know and the ways you use to make sense of them. Because the words are within the context of the quote, have students use the context to help them figure out the meaning of unknown words.

When discussing the meaning of the quote and how it relates to your students, have them use their new vocabulary in conversations. Have students look for targeted vocabulary in books they are reading or during read alouds. Because my students truly used the word lists I gave them for the 100 most frequently used words and the coveted one from the fifth-grade teachers, I felt they would be receptive to creating another list of words used by famous Black people.

Inside the Classroom, January 19

At every teacher gathering, student behavior is the primary subject of discussion and complaints. Each teacher attempts to control behavior in a different way. One ties behavior to academics. She paddles her students for problems they missed on a math test, one whack for each missed question. Another teacher alternates Army sergeant tactics with humor and love. I have found that being positive works best, but I must be firm. In fact, I must not allow any misbehavior or the students take clear advantage. Along with using positive speech, smiling and laughing, humor has worked very well for me. Planning for every minute of my children's time in class also works. It is important to keep them busy on meaningful work. The Study Folder and the two library books my children keep at their desks are to keep them engaged in learning after they have completed their assignments

Whatever strategies are used, no one to my knowledge has found a magic solution that works for all students. What works for one may not work for another. Behavioral management is the number one stressor experienced by teachers and the number one topic discussed during faculty meetings.

This morning, we went to a school-wide magic show that my students loved. However, once they returned to class, they became upset that our routine had been disrupted. "We didn't do the calendar." and "We didn't write in our journals." were two routines they missed the most. Because they sat so long during the magic show, some legitimately had to use the bathroom. Others took advantage of this opportunity to leave the classroom to join their friends all during the time I wanted to talk with my students about the magic show. The constant appeals to use the bathroom upset my teaching schedule which, in turn, made me grouchy. Yet, as the adult in the room, I should have been able to handle disruptions to my routines better than I did. Next time, I will plan to have a bathroom break immediately after we have gone to a school program.

Teacher-to-Teacher Commentary

Behavior continues to raise its ugly head! Here we are midway through the school year, and we are all coping with behavioral problems. I know we have all tried different ways to help our students so forgive me if in my research I state the obvious. Expert teachers look for causes of behavior rather than simply reacting to behavioral problems as they occur (Terada 2021). It is essential to look beneath the behavior to understand what triggers children to misbehave. Is it boredom, frustration, confusion, something that happened outside the classroom? Students enter the classroom each day after experiencing a myriad of issues that originated at home and with their peers. We expect them to shed these feelings at the classroom door and be attentive participants in the lessons. Furthermore, students come to class carrying emotional loads of their own insecurities and deep-seated needs to impress their classmates.

Teachers at district meetings have supplied ideas to manage behavior. The following are bits and pieces of advice from the teachers that I have tried to use during the day. Some you may have heard before, but I hope you find something that is helpful:

1. Class management is a part of teaching, expect it.
2. Give students some ownership by involving them in the planning of behavior rules and procedures.
3. Behavioral expectations must be clear and understood by students and parents.
4. Be brief. Avoid long lectures and explanations.
5. Do not embarrass a student; address more serious problems privately.
6. When angry, cool off before making decisions or addressing an issue with your student.
7. Never call the student names. Haim Ginott (2003) advises that teachers criticize the action, not the child. For example, if the child's desk is messy, avoid name calling such as, "You are so messy." Instead, attack the desk. This desk is a mess!"
8. Focus on solutions together.

Above all, don't give up! The lives of your students are at stake. Keep looking for ways to promote good behavior necessary for learning.

Inside the Classroom, January 20

The children are engaged in one of three math groups each day. One is taught by my assistant, another is taught by me, and one is an independent center with no direct supervision. We have had some success with the independent center giving me hope that the children can become self-directed. I have so many plans for my centers. I want to find space for an Estimation Station where the children can learn how to estimate numbers, a Writing Center with different sizes of paper, story ideas, word lists, and a chart showing the proper formation of letters. I want to create centers for science and social studies where students learn to use maps and learn about their community. I want to embrace the unit approach where learning in the different content areas is connected to a theme such as dinosaurs, plants, farm animals, and so forth. I have done some of that for the centers the students use in the Special Centers during the last 30 minutes of the day. I need to factor in a time to help my slower students learn reading and mathematics.

Teacher-to-Teacher Commentary

The conundrum of how to group students, whether you group low, middle, and high performing students together, or have a mixed group where the lower and middle performing children can learn from each other is frequently debated by educators. I found that mixed ability groups were difficult for some of my lower performing children because they had not yet learned necessary basic skills. Instead, the more proficient members of the group took over. When I asked a proficient member in a higher grade whether helping students struggling in math helped him, he replied, "I have no idea how to teach them." This insight into students tutoring students led me to think that the advanced students should be tutored on ways to teach specific basic skills.

Because my students had different needs, I chose to group by ability. However, this led to problems. With three separate groups: low, middle, and high, I had to be in three places at once to check on students' progress during the time I was teaching one of the groups. Too many times I have observed teachers who sat with one group and rarely checked on what the other students were accomplishing.

In a research-based article on reading groups Sparks (2022) found that students in mixed ability and high groups improved their vocabulary. To communicate in groups for reading, social studies and the STEAM subjects (science, technology, engineering, art, and mathematics), students working in groups were able to hear and speak more words in context. Not surprisingly, more vocabulary was used and learned by students in similar ability groups. The research also showed that teacher modeling and guidance helped students. An obvious, but important fact, Sparks found, was that one-on-one teaching was twice as effective as group work.

Earlier research by Hall and Burns (2017) focused on reading, but their recommendations could also easily be applied to STEAM and social studies. "Catch them early" was shown to have more powerful effects on later student learning. This simple fact may lead you to think that not only catching students early leads to academic improvement, but they have less time to develop negative thoughts about the subject/s they are struggling with. They found that targeting specific skills had greater outcomes than trying to teach multiple skills. Other considerations include group size, time, and the credentials of the adults leading the groups. Many schools use grandparents, parents, and teacher assistants. Though well-intentioned, they are most effective when trained by the teacher on what and how to teach.

Our conclusion is that good students benefit by being around good students and poor students benefit by being around good students. The problem? We don't have enough good students to go around.

Inside the Classroom, January 21

At a faculty meeting Ms. Wrigley was very upset about what the President of the State Board of Education said about administrators. He wants the administrators of each school to be held accountable. If after one or two years the school is still failing, the principal is to be removed, followed the next year by the superintendent and the school board. Our principal said that we would be in trouble if the rest of the board listens to him. I think it is a great idea! Nothing will be accomplished by administrators who are themselves inept, and in my mind, thriving on power. All the platitudes of helping the students are mouthed, but not supported by actions that reflect best practices, are empty. Ruling by negativism, paddling children, bypassing teachers' opinions, and making decisions about students with little to no data, it is no wonder our principal did not take standardized tests seriously. If we must inflate our grades to avoid failing any of our students, the results from an objective measure of student learning, standardized tests, are worthless. The placement of students is done at the whim of the principal and is not based on testing, observation, or other objective criteria.

Teacher-to-Teacher Commentary

Who is accountable for student learning? Typically, I have read that the teachers are accountable, but running a school falls to the school and district administrators as well. So far, the commentaries have focused on the teachers and students. Now, we come to the head of the district and school, the superintendent and principal. The superintendent is responsible for administering to the health and safety of the students, implementing federal programs, transportation, finance, and gifted and special education programs. The principal is responsible for implementing the demands of the superintendent and coping directly with the programs within the school. He or she is responsible for overseeing all the people who work with children in a particular school. This includes the teachers, teacher assistants, coaches, janitorial staff, cafeteria staff, and school nurse.

We had a first-year principal who, even with a master's degree in administration, was ineffective due to her constant threatening pronouncements. Though harshly spoken negative comments were made frequently by many of the teachers, they were the ones who complained loudly when they were the recipient of such comments by the principal.

Inside the Classroom, January 24

Today, I taught for the first time without my usual planning notes. I have always made weekly plans, and each morning before I went to school, I reviewed my plans and wrote even more detailed plans for the day. This not only refreshed me, but it helped me think through all that I want to teach and how to use the materials I had gathered for each lesson the day before. A more experienced teacher can omit this but I have found this step very helpful. However, last night I had no time to review my notes so today I had to rely on the plans I had written last week. The day went well, but I did not feel as secure or smooth in my teaching. I am continuing to see the very valuable benefit of copious planning to avoid having the students do the same things each day.

Teacher-to-Teacher Commentary

Be prepared! Over-confidence leads to a let-down in planning. If anything, by now you know your students, their behaviors, needs, and academic performance. Don't take shortcuts with your planning, it should change as your students do. One teacher bragged that she wrote the dates in her plan book in pencil so she could simply erase and change the date to the current one. She used the same plans for many years. She pulled one over on the principal but did nothing to help her students whose needs varied from year-to-year.

Now that the students have been back from Christmas break, recharge your lessons. Include the wisdom you have gathered about the academic and behavioral needs of your students and seek plenty of ways to vary your lessons to meet their needs. Seek alternative ways to include movement that supports your objectives. In other words, you have a fresh start!

Inside the Classroom, January 25

We have been working on character traits this past week. Sadly, I have seen the beginnings of many delinquent type traits including fighting, bad language, lack of courtesy, and theft in my own room. Individually the children are wonderfully charming and good. As a group, many negative traits dominate. Therefore, I have been displaying a character word once every few days and we discuss it and relate it to two of their favorite Black heroes, Martin Luther King and Tiger Woods. The first word we worked on was "honesty." The children were very interested and have made a real effort to tell the truth. I sometimes wondered whether they are deliberately doing something wrong so they can tell the truth and get praise for their honesty. I hope this doesn't backfire on me!

Today I posted a 100 Acts of Kindness chart low enough so the children can reach it. Each time they have done an act of kindness for another child, they can write their name and a brief description of their kind act. Many children have used this chart which makes me feel good. In a sense, it is my students' act of kindness toward me.

Teacher-to-Teacher Commentary

As a teacher, it is easy to feel possessive about your students, I did. It is not that I didn't trust the parents, but my primary focus was on teaching my students, whom I thought of as "my children." Once it dawned on me that my children's character traits were first shaped before they even entered my classroom, I saw that my solo attempts to help them develop good character traits were missing critical collaboration with the parents, extended family, and other caregivers.

Though you will think of other character traits important to your class, these are the ones I aimed for in my first-grade class: respect, honesty, self-control, goal setting, and optimism. By identifying and working on the traits you want your students to learn rather than addressing them as the need arises, gives you an opportunity to work with parents to plan ways to instill them in your students. Too often, it was easy to complain about students' behavior rather than identify the character traits that got in the way of learning and socializing. By working on individual traits, you have an opportunity to involve the parents so you can work as a team. Pick a trait you want to teach and nurture. Then focus on it.

On the flip side of parental collaboration, an approach to helping students learn character traits is expressed by a mother who enrolled her young American child in a Chinese school in Shanghai. Character traits described in Lenora Chu's book *Little Soldiers* are single-handedly forced on the children with no home-school collaboration. Teaching character traits begins early and continues throughout the grades. Chu became involved in the Chinese school system through her little boy, Rainer, age four, after moving to China and enrolling him in a Chinese school that demanded respect and conformity. For example, he was taught how to sit in his chair, keeping his back straight, feet on the floor, and hands on his knees. When the teacher entered the classroom, Rainer, along with the rest of the class immediately rose and stood at attention and did not sit until told to by the teacher. Rainer was forced to eat food he didn't like, even if it meant the teacher forcibly put it in his mouth and made him swallow. If children did not follow the rules, they were expelled. Rainer's parents strongly considered taking him out of the Chinese school and enrolling him in an American school with laxer behavioral standards until they saw how the rigid approach helped him develop character traits of respect and attention to learning. While this method is extreme, it did produce results.

Back to the American schools. Research has shown that parental involvement in character development leads to greater achievement (Perry-Jenkins, 2023). Ideally, parents and teachers work together to build desired character traits. Of these traits, optimism was a trait I should have focused on daily. Helping young children learn the trait of optimism, an "I can do it" mentality, will serve them well as they go through life. In hindsight, I wish I had embedded positive thinking into my daily objectives, something like, "Today I will write my best story," "I will solve ten mathematics problems." or , "I will learn six of my spelling words." You could post one or more behavioral objectives such as, "Today I will help a friend." At the end of the day, pass out a strip of paper and have students write one goal they met and drop it in a box as they leave the classroom. They can choose whether or not to write their name on the slip of paper. Designate a special place in the classroom to post the goals students met that day. During the opening part of the next day, go over the goals the students met before asking them to set new goals. The focus on goals promotes positive thinking and a mindset of success which helps to replace the negative thoughts that have plagued my students who have had a history of failure. There is so much I plan to do next year!

Inside the Classroom, January 26

We have reading placement tests sitting on our shelves and so far, we have not received permission or written instructions on how to administer them. This is a test that is to be standardized across the district yet we have not been given a specific day and time to give them. The tests, given early enough, will provide valuable information to the teachers on the strengths and weaknesses of the students' reading progress.

Teacher-to-Teacher Commentary

Both formative and summative assessments are important to gauge how well students are learning and how much they have learned.

Formative (ongoing) assessment is to inform the students and the teacher about strengths and weaknesses exhibited by the students as they are learning. Rubrics, checklists, anecdotal notes, daily or weekly written work, low-stakes tests and quizzes, and portfolios are some of the ways to gather data on students during the time they are learning so teachers can diagnose problems and celebrate successes with their students.

Summative (formal) assessment provides information about the durability and generalizability of the learning. Have the students remembered and can they use it in other situations? It is important to find out what students have learned at the midpoint and end of a unit or chapter. The assessment must be matched to learning objectives to provide teachers with relevant information on the effectiveness of the methods, pacing, and materials they used. Summative assessment not only informs the students and teachers of the progress of learning, it is used to provide quarterly feedback to parents and caregivers on the students' level of learning. High-stakes tests is a summative assessment used to determine promotion, and retention. A parting thought: avoid negative thoughts and negative people. Focus all your energy on helping your students.

Inside the Classroom, January 27

Today I tried something new for an upcoming standardized math test. I went over the sections of a practice test with the children and we reviewed the concepts that were tested. I then let the children work on the test at their own pace. I walked around and helped with the directions. It was a disaster. The children could not or would not follow the directions. Two cheated and some did not finish. I plan to give more of the types of problems that were on the first practice test and then give it again. I am puzzled as the concepts on the practice test are fairly simple: counting by ones, fives, and tens, greater and less than, ordinal numbers, and basic addition and subtraction problems, all concepts I had taught prior to the practice test. The children seemed to understand the concepts, many even appeared bored saying it is easy, yet they could not perform on a test that was given to them without step-by-step guidance through the directions. Perhaps I should use more worksheets to help students learn how to follow directions. My children like them, but I have tried to keep worksheets at a minimum, focusing as much as I can on active learning activities.

Teacher-to-Teacher Commentary

At least, the format of the test became familiar to the students. Imagine that in the near future, we may use computer-oriented assessments. All of us have tried to navigate through websites trying to respond affirmatively to directions and all of us have experienced the confusion that occurs when the directions on the website are vague, obscure, mixed with computer jargon, or even contradictory. Machine-oriented test taking is here. We must get the students ready to take these standardized tests not only using paper and pencil, but also by following instructions on a computer screen. Technology could be a *barrier* to children, especially children living in poverty to demonstrate what they know. We must teach them to overcome that barrier.

Websites are designed by people who are familiar with terms and jargon that may not be familiar with the customers, so *everything* must be explained. One of the best ways to assess the design of such a website is to have a noncomputer-oriented customer try to get what he wants without assistance. The quality of a website is determined by the ease that the customer has when successfully ordering what he wants. Only when the technology is mastered… not just superficially understood… but mastered, will the student's knowledge of the subject matter be assessed properly. The computer screen must be as familiar as the worksheet and the keyboard as familiar as a pencil. The directions should be written without jargon and as simple as possible. Otherwise, what we're assessing is technology knowledge, not content knowledge.

Inside the Classroom, January 28

Today some of my children were especially bad. De'Andre, Julious, Mikal, Jordan, and Cade were in trouble the whole day. Cade even flicked his finger behind my back when I made him sit down. I sent a formal letter home with a threat to have Mr. Goodson, the vice-principal, contact his mother if I didn't get a signed note in return. Cade appeared very contrite, saving a place for me at lunch. He even stroked my arm when he was apologizing, but his behavior did not change. The children know I won't paddle them. It goes against everything I thought about discipline. Not paddling may be contributing to the behavior problems because the children feel they have nothing to fear. However, these same children are paddled frequently on the days I am absent from school and I don't see a change in their behavior. I am going to try Ms. Miller's marbles. Students get two marbles at the end of a day if they do not have their name written down for misbehaving. At the end of the week, the children count their marbles and receive a prize if they collected 10 marbles. I can't imagine this would work, and already envision a lot of problems, but it is worth a chance.

I talked to De'Andre's mother today. She is very concerned about what we can do to help him with his behavior. Like me, she has noticed an increase in misbehavior that includes lying and blaming others for his wrongdoing. I plan to write a letter recommending that De'Andre be evaluated for emotional problems in hopes that we can find ways to help him. De'Andre has an older sister who has been in jail for at least two years for trying to kill her mother. Meanwhile, his mother is taking care of his sister's five-year old daughter. He comes from a very caring, but complicated home situation.

Teacher-to-Teacher Commentary

The book, *Black Children*, by Janice E. Halle states that Black children are used to spontaneous speech and movement. She used services at the Black church as an example of spontaneity. When I think of it, if this is the dominant culture experienced by my children, they are indeed going to have a problem when told to sit and speak only when spoken to. It is too bad, but whenever I try to give my children an opportunity to talk and move freely, some abuse this by becoming loud, off task, and eventually pushing, hitting, or fighting. Another trait that greatly disturbs me is my students' propensity to tattle on one another and to laugh at children who get into trouble or who are experiencing difficulty. I must do more to teach character traits.

As for the marble idea, I tried my mentor's idea of awarding marbles for good behavior. Though my students wanted to collect marbles that went toward a prize, they really did not want them badly enough to earn them through good behavior. Furthermore, this method caused distractions. The children were always dropping their marbles on their way to plunking them into their cans that sat on the windowsill. Overall, this has possibilities for teaching math, but both my mentor and I gave up on this idea after just a couple of weeks. The distractions caused by the marbles were as bad as the behaviors we were trying to change.

Inside the Classroom, January 31

Today's low point came when one of my children threw up in the hallway outside our classroom. I told the children to go into the room and put their heads down until I came. The classroom door was open and I was right outside, but out of sight. When I looked in three of my children were jumping on their chairs, and according to one child, Julious had been "feeling Angelina on the butt." I revoked privileges for those involved. Sadly, the children whose privileges have been revoked are becoming used to this and it does not have the impact I had hoped for. I must think of something that makes an impact on these children. I told my class that they could not even be trusted to help me when I needed them and I was very disappointed. My little lecture did not produce any noticeable effects; the offending students did not seem to care.

Teacher-to-Teacher Commentary

My children's reaction to an emergency of a sick child puzzled me because when a little girl with visible physical disabilities was mainstreamed into our classroom for socialization, my children outdid themselves vying to hold her hand and help her at lunch. An older student who looked as though he belonged in high school was enrolled in special education at our school. My children and those from other classrooms all trailed around him at recess vying to hold his hand as he quietly walked around the playground. Where was their empathy for helping a sick classmate and friend?

My angry lecture did not work. Revoking privileges did not work. Praising students who sat quietly did not work. Despite the contrite faces of the offending students, I was sure they would do the same thing again when given a chance. Teaching classroom rules is one thing, teaching kindness and empathy is going to be much more difficult. Do my students even know what the words kindness and empathy mean? By the way, which comes first kindness and empathy or empathy and kindness, and does it matter?

The Random Acts of Kindness Foundation (2024) advises that teachers should actively teach six core concepts of kindness and empathy: respect, caring, inclusiveness, integrity, responsibility, and courage. These traits must be, taught, retaught, and reinforced by modeling. Because the sick child incident came during the time we were engrossed in Martin Luther King's birthday and right before Black History month, I now see an opportunity to connect the core concepts to the actions of Black heroes.

Another way to help students learn the meaning of kindness and empathy is to teach them to follow the popular idiom, "Pay it Forward." Those who receive an act of kindness have to pay it forward by being kind to someone else. Discuss ways to "Pay it Forward." In addition to these discussions, use books about empathy and kindness such as *The Kindness Quilt by* N.E. Wallace and *Have You Filled a Bucket Today?* by C. McCloud.

Today's online articles and web sites offer a wealth of research-based and practical information on ways to teach empathy and kindness. Ackerman, (2017) has written 40 ways to teach empathy. Wilson, D. (2017) presented four strategies. The following are the three steps I would have found helpful for my class:

1. Provide examples of empathy and kindness. We could begin by having students revisit the 100 Acts of Kindness chart described in the January 25th entry and discuss ways they showed empathy and kindness to each other.

2. Have students look back at their behavior during their classmate's time of need and describe the effects of their actions.

3. Brainstorm ways to understand the feelings of their classmates in need of help and ways they could have demonstrated kindness.

Chapter 5
February-March – Middle of Winter

Inside the Classroom, February 3

I've begun something new as consequence to bad behavior that seems to satisfy both my children and me. When my class lapses into talking, especially when it interrupts my lesson, I have them copy words from the board. Yesterday, they copied each of the spelling words and wrote sentences for them. Today they wrote contractions from their reading story. One interesting side note: One of the contractions was he'll. I was a little nervous about introducing it as I was sure some of my children who had an eye for cuss words would react to it. I had no need to worry. I made sure the apostrophe was clearly marked. The spelling and pronouncing "he'll" went right over the heads of my children. However, when they heard the word "hail," many of my boys began saying the word "hell" and laughed. At the first-grade level, written words are still so new to the children that they don't recognize "he'll" when they see it, but they sure hear similar sounds. Anyway, back to having the children write as a consequence for poor behavior. The writing keeps them quiet and working. When carefully planned and not just busy work, it furthers their education as they pay the price for inattentive behavior. The children groan when told they must do it, but then something inexplicable happens. Many do not want to stop writing! They are proud of all they have written and are eager to share their work with me. One little boy kissed me and said he loved me, the other children seemed happier than usual.

My children love to do work, but they can't sit still to listen to the directions or explanations. Having them write is far better than having them keep their heads down, frequent stern lectures from me, or trying to plow through and teach a class that is restless. After writing spelling words from the board and writing sentences for each one, I had high spelling grades for most of my students. The children who do not cause trouble have the option of writing words from the board or working in activities in special centers. Surprisingly, some of my well-behaved students chose to write.

Teacher-to-Teacher Commentary

When children keep their heads down, they no longer disrupt the class, but they are not learning. By now, they should have learned to follow the familiar behavioral expectations. My mentor has her disruptive students sit in a different classroom and has offered this technique to me. However, though she is an excellent teacher, we are at different places in the curriculum which could bore or frustrate my students. Perhaps it would be interesting to switch classrooms during reading or any other content area lesson, but this must be done with prior planning on our part. Team teaching is something to consider.

It is important to keep up with the duration of the time related to language and behavior. You have your precious students eight hours a day, 180 days a year. The rest of the time the language they hear and the behavioral expectations of their peers occur outside of your influence. Keep current with social media, watch popular television programs, and listen to current music for language and behaviors your students of all ages are exposed to today.

Inside the Classroom, February 8

Our district lives and dies by the tests, yet the testing procedure is in disarray. Tomorrow we are to give all first-grade classes a state practice test. Not even the first-grade team leader knows the test format or directions. We have never seen the state test nor have we been told what was to be tested. My assistant and I sharpened 25 pencils in preparation, but I really wonder if we will give the test tomorrow. Because there was no set of third-grade practice tests, the third-grade teachers had to administer second-grade practice tests to their students without directions on how to administer them. It would be interesting, and perhaps confidence building to give students tests one grade level below theirs. This would be a great way for the students to practice taking a standardized test and find that the questions and answers are below their level. Wow! Except for the cost, and perhaps the confidentiality of the test content, this is could be a confidence boosting experience and a way for students to practice using the format of the test on familiar content.

Teacher-to-Teacher Commentary

Testing, particularly standardized testing is an emotional issue. Educators rail against the supposed waste of time and money that our "obsession" with testing consumes. As a classroom teacher, it is true that considerable time is spent administering standardized tests. But it is important to remember the reason for testing in the first place. Tests are supposed to measure the knowledge of the student. They ought to be valuable tools in the hands of a competent teacher. The results can guide the teacher on the content their students have mastered and content that needs improving. Sure, the testing costs money and time, but what's the alternative? Not testing? Aside from this absurdity, taxpayers are hungry for an indication that the school is actually doing its job. Tests, however imperfect, do measure a student's knowledge and progress. Tests are not going away, nor should they.

The literature is replete with instances of cultural bias in testing, cheating (by both student and teacher), high prices of standardized testing, and time consumption. When these criticisms are valid, they should be acknowledged by those in authority to improve the efficiency and effectiveness of testing, rather than ignoring the information. (Penn State 2019).

Inside the Classroom, February 18

We had a staff development day to learn about a new computerized reading program, Academy of Reading. Normally, I look forward to these because I always learn something I can take back to my class. Even when I was a substitute, I stayed after school to attend the meetings that had a speaker. However, this meeting was boring and long. The teacher who was teaching us how to use the program knew slightly more than we did, and our time at the computer was not long enough for us to really get into the program and understand all that it does. The company claims that after 25 hours of computer instruction, a child's reading level will be increased to a 2.5 grade level.

This is typical and speaks ill of the organization of our district and school. This program has been loaded into our computers since before Christmas, but we are just now learning how to use it. During the meeting, my mentor and I tried to understand how to use the program, but we both had problems. We were unsure as to the content of the program until we read about it online and learned that it covered the important core skills needed by young readers: phonemic awareness, phonics, fluency, vocabulary, and comprehension. At this point in the school year, our students had learned phonemic awareness and phonics. We had already begun to focus on vocabulary, fluency, and comprehension. It is very difficult to find time to sit and explore the new computer program because we can only stay one hour after the children leave before they turn off the inside lights and lock the outside doors. During that hour, I am cleaning up, trying to set up for the next day, making learning aids, hanging up children's work on the bulletin board, and so forth. In the winter when it gets dark so early, without lights it is difficult to stay later than 4:30 to learn how to use the computer program because the hallways are dark and little light comes into the classroom through the windows. When leaving school after 4:30 we find the parking lot has begun to fill up with teenagers loitering, smoking, and drinking.

Teacher-to-Teacher Commentary

The access to computers has grown exponentially in the United States since the late 1900's and early 2000's. To make sure K-12 students have access to computers for learning, many school districts loan computers to their students. Some districts have no fee for students in kindergarten through fifth grade, though their use is restricted to classroom use. From grades 6-12, there is a $50 dollar fee that enables students to take their computer home. This fee is waived for students who qualify for free and reduced lunch. Students can use computers in most U.S. libraries. Before the advent of the popular use of computers, teachers like me, had to cope with computer problems in addition to learning a new reading program. It was terribly frustrating. Even working with other teachers, we finally gave up using a computer-based reading program that could have helped our students. Hopefully, this is not such an overwhelming problem for teachers today.

Inside the Classroom, February 21

Another Monday. I am always sad to leave my husband to return to my apartment near my school. Once I see my children it is easy to get back into my life as a teacher. This is not to say that teaching is easy, the children are active and I spend more time than I'd like keeping everyone on task. One of my new ways, when I don't have recess duty, is to keep offending students in at recess and give them extra work. I've waited a long time to try this as I always thought that the students who misbehave need recess to play with their friends and, hopefully, be a little tired when they return to class. However, they return to class as rambunctious as ever. I keep trying new ways to help my children's behavior problems and hope this one will work.

Joy and Heartbreak

Teacher-to-Teacher Commentary

A note about losing recess. The literature on teaching tells us not to revoke a student's recess. They need time to run off their energy. Therefore, as a last resort, I began revoking recess, but I usually took two to three minutes or no longer than half of their 20-minute recess away. The two-to-three-minute delay was effective because the children missed opportunities to bring out the balls, jump ropes, and large chalk. Also, the swings and slides quickly filled up before they could get there.

When I tried out my plan to keep students in at recess and give them extra work, it was successful, but not in the way I thought. The extra work is either copying spelling words or writing me a letter telling me what they have done and how they will change their behavior. It is perverse, but the children love the extra work! They are proud of all the writing they do, and some do not want to stop! What am I to do, tell the children if they do not behave, I will send them out to recess?

When I had recess duty, I had the offending students bring out their tablets and pencils and sit next to the playground. I kept them busy writing and doing school work. These children loved sitting and doing work even as they saw their friends play. Some kept on working even when I told them they could join their friends. There are always surprises in store for me!!

One thing I learned by being in the trenches is that there are no simple answers to problems related to classroom management. Before returning to teaching, I felt I had the answers to just about every problem my university students could present. Ha!

Inside the Classroom, February 22

Bad behavior masks the fact that I am dealing with a young and vulnerable population. The very boys who fight in the bathroom, sit and flex their muscles during class, steal pencils from others, are easily reduced to tears if they perceive they have been unfairly singled out and punished. They are also quick to want to help in minor ways such as picking up a book or piece of chalk I dropped during my lesson. One of my toughest boys, who had been retained twice, in response to my writing a star on the board when the class was good said, "That makes me happy!" Another tough guy said, "During the weekend I missed school." These same boys loved it when I gave them our stuffed classroom dog to hold at their seats if they were working hard and were kind to other students. I was humbled and vow to use more positive acknowledgments of good student behavior.

De'Andre, one of my rambunctious boys with physical problems, jumped up during a lesson saying he had an idea. He walked to each row, we have five, and said I could call the first row Monday, the second row Tuesday, and so forth. He was elated when I used his idea and referred to the rows by the names of the days of the week. He said, "Ms. Holmes, you used my idea!" This single event did not cure bad behavior but letting him name the rows put a sparkle in his eye.

The same child who had such a successful time by having his idea accepted in class ran into a snag at the close of the day. We had been reading a Dr. Seuss story, "The Foot Book." In the story many types of feet are described, quick feet, trick feet, tired feet, happy feet, and so forth. As he left our classroom, he was half skipping and jumping. He was still close to my class and was not hurting anything or even out of control so I commented, "De'Andre, I see you have happy feet!" He turned to smile when a large hand roughly grabbed him on the shoulder. It was a teaching assistant acting as a hall monitor who shouted at him to get into line. So much for those happy feet! Children are not talked to before and after school; they are yelled at for the slightest provocation by the hall assistants.

Teacher-to-Teacher Commentary

At this point in the year, some of my children had earned their reputations for disrupting their class or failing to follow directions. Their reputations, already established early in life, had followed them from teacher to teacher. They were infamous! They were remembered by their previous teachers for their out-of-control behavior. The tendency was to focus on deficits rather than the children's strengths. Looking into my children's eyes after catching them breaking a classroom or school rule helped me see that I was dealing with vulnerable children. It was too easy to focus on their bad behaviors rather than the individual traits that endured them to me. If you look only at bad behavior, you will be sure to find it. However, lurking beneath the surface are the hardships and failures my children had experienced before they came into the classroom. Don't expect the worst from a child.

It is helpful to identify individual behaviors that your students are likely to exhibit. Self-regulation includes self-motivation where a student seeks to meet recognizable goals. For example, one little boy had difficulty writing letters properly. When he showed me a list of four or five lower-case "a's"' I showed him the one I thought was best by writing a little star over it. I asked him if he agreed and if he did, he could write his own star. Other times, I let him choose the letter he wrote best and let him write a little star over it. We discussed why it was a well-written letter, or why I did not choose it. This simple procedure kept him focused on writing the best possible letters that he could. It was only a five-minute lesson, but he was willing to work on his handwriting.

In an article by Smolleck & Duffy (2017) the authors identified common behavioral problems they have seen in multiple classrooms. They found that the most common problems were students' inability to complete tasks, anger, aggression, attention seeking from the teacher and peers, and their home lives. Do these sound familiar? The authors found that noting when misbehaviors occurred and seeking solutions to prevent them helped teachers find ways for their students to control their behavior. Though taking time to talk through a problem with a student pulls you away from the rest of the class, it provides an important dialogue to help the student. This proactive, rather than a reactive approach to misbehavior lets the students know you care about them and that they CAN succeed. Furthermore, by talking through a problem, you will gain insights about your students, their strengths, and areas of weakness. Armed with this information, you are in a much better place to help them.

Inside the Classroom, February 23

I learned the hard way to not to rush the curriculum. I had followed the pace of the lessons on money in the textbook. I was to introduce pennies followed by nickels, dimes, and quarters. We had been counting by fives and tens for most of the year so I thought that counting by nickels and dimes would be easy. Not so! I should have realized that the very abstract nature of money would make it difficult for most children to relate what they knew about skip counting to the counting of money. The children were very frustrated, and so was I. I asked my friend and mentor, Ms. Miller in the classroom next to mine who said that she spends at least three weeks with just pennies and nickels. I plan to slow the pace of my lessons on money and review the concepts of addition and subtraction, counting by 5s and 10s before applying them to money. It is essential to break down any lesson that is difficult for the children into small chunks.

Today Ms. Miller came into my room feeling very down as her students did not do well on a math test on money. I was so very impressed by her attitude. She felt like a "failure" because her students did not learn. This is the attitude of an exceptional teacher. It is so easy to blame the students, rather than take the responsibility.

Teacher-to-Teacher Commentary

Skip counting supports learning of number patterns, a precursor of place value, multiplication, and division. These skills can be directly taught and developed through hands-on activities including the money game. It is important to consider what students must know, do, and understand to learn the values of coins and connect them to skip counting. They are counting cents, not coins, and some coins are worth more than others. The application of skip counting to the values of pennies, nickels, and dimes is not obvious to a first grader. Initially, students may be able to skip count forward and backward without thinking and they can count the number of coins they have without knowing their value. What is learned in one area often doesn't transfer automatically to another area in the mind of a child. For help on what to teach at each grade level, consult the National Council of Teachers of Mathematics (NCTM, 2000) and the Common Core State Standards Initiative, (CCSS, 2021) for mathematics.

My mentor and I relied on active learning where students could explore and discover basic mathematics concepts. If I could do it again, I would first follow the standards to help me sequence my lessons. Then I would teach the value of the coins, have students group their coins by value, and use skip counting to determine how much money they earned in the math game. They would find that skip counting enables them to count things quickly. For example, when counting their nickels to determine how much money they have, they can count by fives. These activities were an excellent way for my students to apply and further their knowledge. You could argue that the early activities actually promoted interest, and you would be right. But at some point, they had to connect what was happening mathematically while engaged in the money game and skip counting activities. Many of my students were too young and inexperienced to make these explicit connections on their own.

Today you have a research-based roadmap for teaching and learning through the Standards at your fingertips. At each level of learning, have your students explain what they did to solve the problems. These diagnostic procedures are as necessary for teachers to treat learning problems as it is for physicians to prescribe a treatment for illness. First comes the diagnosis, then comes the treatment! Diagnosis of student understanding can occur at any time during the mathematics lessons whether they are based on exploration, games and activities, or direct instruction.

Inside the Classroom, February 25

Next week we will be giving some kind of practice test to our first-grade students. I like the idea of practice tests as they will give me advance notice of how my children are doing, an idea of some of the skills that are emphasized and give my children an opportunity to practice using the testing format. In my mind, "teaching to the test" is beneficial to students when it is a part of a total curriculum. My children must learn how to follow directions, engage in test taking strategies, and learn the basic skills needed to answer the questions. Teaching to the test is only a problem for poorly written tests that are not testing what the curriculum is teaching. In well-constructed tests, this is not a problem.

Teacher-to-Teacher Commentary

Testing students at any level is important. Teachers can use what is commonly referred to as low-stakes tests, meaning they are for information and diagnostic purposes, rather than more serious issues such as promotion and retention. Young children in grades K-2 are just learning to read and write at varying degrees. Written tests, even short ones, may be difficult for them to read and express their knowledge through writing. At the beginning of the year, and continuing with my struggling students, I used a lot of oral tests for diagnostic purposes. I listened for their vocabulary and the clarity of their answers. Even though oral tests require a lot of time, I found it helpful to ask my students oral questions before giving them a short-written test. By doing this I could check for comprehension of the question and the degree they know the subject matter. The written tests provided me with a record of the students' performance that I could show the student, parents, and use to base my teaching. It is best to emphasize the positive by setting realistic goals students can meet and celebrate their success. Each day, I had my students write two or three goals they wanted to accomplish that day. With my students' help, at the end of the day, we checked off the ones they met and celebrated their success with stickers, high-fives, and cheers.

Tests written by textbook publishers given at the end of a unit provide valuable information that summarized what individual students learned throughout the unit. Low test scores throughout the year can ultimately affect promotion and retention. Standardized tests given toward the end of the year are used to determine how schools in each district are performing. The least advantaged schools feel the most pressure (Berwick, 2019). Poor test results have an effect on the community. Parents seek to live in a district with high performing schools. The mayor of the small town adjacent to our school literally begged us to do better so he could attract more businesses to the area.

Inside the Classroom, February 28

Something very serious has occurred in my first-grade class. I was told by a student that Julious and Angelina sought each other out and touched each other when I was not looking. This occurred in the classroom library center where I had blocked off part of the center with a bookcase to provide a quiet welcoming place to read. A simple consequence was that I moved the bookcase so I could see all places in my classroom. A more serious consequence to the students was to separate them during free time, group work, and at lunch in addition to telling them why they should not touch one another.

Later that day, Julious, De'Andre, and Delon got into a lot of trouble on their way to speech class. Before they left class, I gave them a pep talk on how to act and dismissed them with a hall pass. Apparently, as soon as I closed the door to my classroom, they raced full speed down the hall. Ms. Miller, another first-grade teacher, stopped them and gave another pep talk on how to walk in the hall. Immediately after she dismissed them, they once again ran down the hall to the speech teacher's room where they acted terribly in speech class. Ms. Taylor, a truly dedicated new teacher, appeared to be at her wit's end with all three of them and took them to the office. Their continued misbehavior ultimately culminated in a paddling of each of them by Mr. Goodson the vice principal.

Teacher-to-Teacher Commentary

By this time of the year, I thought I could trust three of my students, Julious, De'Andre, and Delon to walk quietly down the hall to their speech class. I'm afraid Delon got caught up in the bad behavior of the other two boys whom he looked up to. He has not been a serious problem in class. I felt let down by the three boys. Because they broke my trust in them, I sought answers on how to deal with their behavior. They did not fear consequences of poor behavior or perhaps the consequences were less important than the fun in flouting the rules. I turned to books written by an award-winning 5th grade teacher Rafe Esquith (2003 and 2007) in a critical-needs school in Los Angeles. Not only did his students live in poverty, but many spoke English as a second language, yet he used an almost gentle way of talking to his students. He did not lecture them. Instead, he clearly stated the rules the children were to follow and kept them simple.

Another author, Kennedy-Moore (2018) does a good job describing the effects of lecturing a child who is already misbehaving. She suggested that teachers have the children repeat the rules rather than asking them questions they could not answer such as, "Why did you run down the hall? I could have my boys show me how to walk down the hall. If this doesn't work, I could have asked another teacher to watch them as they practiced walking down the hall and quietly and effusively praise them. In hindsight, I wish I had tried these ways. They might have helped my students learn positive behavior.

Inside the Classroom, March 1

At the beginning of the school year, any little speck of dust or piece of string or paper would occupy my children's attention. Just days ago, I took a small piece of elastic thread from Mikal who had pulled it from his sock and was studying it, tasting it, and playing with it. It made me think that overall, this problem has not been as common as it once had been. I think my children are better than they were about that type of behavior. It is a survival instinct to be attracted to movement so it is understandable when a fly or other small insect captures their attention. However, tugging at a stray thread shows a complete uninterest in the ongoing lesson and will continue to be a problem unless I can address it through prior planning based on my students' interests. Attention to detailed plans can help students maintain focus on the lesson, not a stray thread.

Joy and Heartbreak

Teacher-to-Teacher Commentary

The behavior Mikal showed while quietly playing with a thread from his sock was not bothering anybody but me. During that time, I knew he was not learning. However, his behavior did not warrant a loud embarrassing pronouncement or harsh consequences. It did warrant ways to interest him enough to overpower the thrill of the thread from a sock. The sixty-four-thousand-dollar question is how do you rekindle a student's interest in your lesson? I am sure you have a lot of tricks up your sleeve and I would love to hear them. One way is to learn about the interests of your students and seek to connect them to your lessons. This requires thinking on your feet, not an easy task, but finding a way to lure your student back to the lesson is worth it!

This experience showed that it would be helpful to write an interest inventory for each student at the beginning of the year. Keep this list handy and use it when a sock's thread or a particle of dust has captured one or more of your students' interests. This is easier said than done for teachers in departmentalized classes where they have far more students. Perhaps the students can fill out a simple form you can keep for each of your classes.

All of my children were interested in the accomplishments of famous Black people. Because they have become their heroes, I continued to use them as role models to follow. I connected all their positive character traits to the character traits I want my students to develop. We have discussed and reviewed the deeds and quotes from well-known Black people. The person who continued to be most popular was Dr. Martin Luther King. He was famous for saying that nonviolence is "the guiding light" of the American civil rights movement. In hindsight, I wish I had done more to focus on Martin Luther King's nonviolent approach to solving problems. This would have taken some planning to connect his beliefs and actions to everyday events at school but given the interest and love my students showed toward Dr. King, it would have been helpful.

Inside the Classroom, March 3

At a faculty meeting, our principal was very upset by the lack of discipline she sees in the classrooms and the halls. I think most of her comments were directed to the upper grades, but she did not seem happy with any of us. She stated that children are not the same today as they once were. She said that any teacher who could not control his/her students would be suspended five or six days without pay or until they could control their students. Discipline is a major problem for me and every teacher I have talked to.

Teacher-to-Teacher Commentary

This time it is the teachers who are in trouble. So, this is how it feels to be ruled by fear. It reminds me of an old joke, "You are all suspended until morale improves." Many of the teachers could not afford to lose pay. I felt anger for being swept up in a problem that did not always occur in my class. Though problems with my students were real, there were many times they were hard at work and other times there were just a few who needed discipline. If I could advise my principal, I would suggest she focus on the way many of the teachers and the assistants as hall monitors rudely and hurtfully speak daily to the children. The threats by our principal promoted anger among the teachers.

Can we learn from our reactions to the principal's threats that likely paralleled the reactions of our own students? Did we make our students angry when we lectured and threatened them? Most teachers I worked with had the same problems I did with student behavior. Fearing a loss of pay just adds to their problems. What is missing are workshops or meetings on effective behavioral management. We all learned that day that threats are like gasoline added to a fire that created an even bigger problem.

The need to focus on behavioral management in schools of education was summed up in the article, *When Students are Traumatized, Teachers are Too*. The author, Minero (2017) stated that she was "blindsided by the emotional part of teaching." She emphasized that as a new teacher, she was unprepared to handle the emotions underlying behavioral problems she confronted. Schools of education through their departments of teacher and administrator training should factor into their curricula the complex reasons for student behavior and research-based ways for addressing it.

Inside the Classroom, March 9

Because improvement is so important, I try to find ways I can show my students how much they have improved. De'Andre, the little boy with physical difficulties resulting in drool-smeared messy handwriting sat right next to a boy with excellent handwriting. De'Andre began to cry as he told me he was never going to write neatly. I had saved his writing samples in his portfolio and showed him how he was improving. He looked at me and said, "Ms. Holmes, I am learning, I am learning!"

This experience reminded me of a time one of my student teachers was reviewing alphabet cards with a young child. Each time the child correctly named a letter, the student teacher put the card into one pile and when the child could not correctly name a letter, the student teacher put the card into another pile. The child asked what the two stacks of cards meant. Pointing to the tall stack, the student teacher said, "These are the ones you missed." A positive approach would have been to pick up the small stack and say, "These are all the letters you know! Let's see how many more cards you can add to this stack." Focus on the positive and goal setting. Record learning deficits to guide planning and teaching.

Teacher-to-Teacher Commentary

To help students see their positive gains in learning, it is essential to keep samples of their work, or focus on things they have learned through conversation where students could identify the things that they learned, and the things that are difficult to learn. Students could even help set the goals for the next steps in learning. Of course, you must already know the goals you want your students to master. If the learning goals are too easy, the students will experience less emotional success when they are met. However, for struggling students and, like my students who have been retained, you can begin with goals you know they can reach to provide some level of confidence before making the goals more difficult. Keep the goals difficult enough to work toward them, but achievable.

If you wanted to get creative with goal setting, you could provide a road map for the student to follow with goals written on highway signs. When discussing young students'

Joy and Heartbreak

progress meeting the goals, you could give them a little toy car to move along the map. To be honest, I have never tried the road map method, but with a little imagination, you can probably come up with several ideas to add this and other ways to provide visual information for your students to follow as they work toward meeting their goals.

Chapter 6
April-May – Springtime

Inside the Classroom, April 3

We are well into the school year and discipline continues to be a serious problem for every teacher I have talked to. Many children still do not consider the consequences of their actions. I was looking at their legs while we were eating lunch, and they were constantly moving. In the past, I noticed that children in preschool constantly paced back and forth while talking to me. I felt like I was watching a tennis match while my head moved from side-to-side. Have some first-grade children not outgrown the need to move?

Teacher-to-Teacher Commentary

The need to move and touch things varies with the students' age and background. Older, students who have experienced failure may continue to move and touch things to alleviate anxiety. Some may become restless when they are tired and hungry, while others may act out when they are frustrated during a lesson. A special education instructor at the university suggested giving students who need to move and touch things a way to do so during lessons. For students who constantly have an urge to tap on their desks, she suggested taping a piece of foam on the top of the desk for students to tap. She suggested marking boundaries with blue painters' tape around their desk where students could sit within the boundaries and do their work. This worked reasonably well for some of my students. Unfortunately, my more rambunctious students pushed their space to the limits, moving farther and farther away from the area marked working space. I learned that I shouldn't expect miracles the first time I try something. Just like other behavioral privileges, they must be modeled, taught, and practiced with firm guidelines.

 Here are some other ways you could try to help your students cope with their need to move. Provide squeeze toys that also strengthen their hands. Get a stuffed animal for a class pet and let your students hold and stroke it. Buddy, our class dog, gave my students tactile and calming ways to move. More advanced ways to help calm a student is to use weighted vests or scarves that have a similar effect to gently putting your hands on your students' shoulders and applying light pressure. The vests and scarves should weigh no more than 5-10 percent of the child's weight. Consult with parents and guardians as well as your principal before using them. Never use them as a punishment, only as an intervention. Always use them under your supervision. Make sure children cannot remove the weights from the pockets of the scarf. With proper instruction and guidelines, students should be able to handle the movement comes with these simple interventions

Inside the Classroom, April 12

This was a day of messes. Angelina had a severe nose bleed and dripped a trail of blood from her desk to the tissue box that sat on my desk. During lunch Marcus threw up on the cafeteria floor. Teachers are expected to clean up the mess, so I asked another teacher to watch my class while I went to my classroom for disposable gloves and some special throw-up stuff that resembles shredded wood. This stuff is wonderful! It absorbs all the moisture-laden vomit and smells good. I poured a bunch of it on the mess, got some paper towels and literally picked it up in my glove-protected hand, and put it in the grocery bag I had used to pack my lunch. LaRhonda voluntarily got a mop and finished the job.

At this stage of school, my students had learned to read well enough that they wanted to read their books to me. Though thrilled, I was unable to listen to all the children who wanted to read to me and came up with an idea. Right after school, I talked to the fifth-grade teacher and asked whether she could send six or seven of her students to my class during the last 30 minutes to listen to my students read. I suggested she send her remedial students that could benefit from exposure to books while helping others to read. We set up a schedule for her students to come to my classroom to listen to my students read three times a week.

My friend and mentor, Ms. Miller, has been looking angry and sullen for the past few days. She is upset with her class and said that upon reflection she thought she was being dragged down by the administration. The lack of respect for instructional time and the constant threats and added duties by our principal have made teaching intolerable for her. She speaks up to the principal, but nothing changes. We are all overburdened by a lack of breaks. We eat with our students and recess breaks are at the whim of the duty teachers. If it is the least bit too cold or too hot, or if the grass is wet from a previous rainfall, the duty teachers do not go out. Recess breaks are the only time, except for a once-a-week 20-minute library break that we are not constantly with our students from 7:00 AM to 3:15 PM. During this time, we are spoken to by multitudes of children just about every minute of the day. This leaves little time to set up materials and review our afternoon lesson plans while our students are in the classroom.

Teacher-to-Teacher Commentary

As teachers, how many of you have had disruptions that were no fault of the child? It is almost impossible to get through the year without someone getting hurt, sick, or having a nosebleed. Make sure the necessary supplies for cleaning have not gotten buried somewhere in the back of your cupboard. Review the way you would seek help for serious problems. Model professional behavior toward the child and the ensuing mess that results. Since Covid, the demand for disposable gloves is even more necessary, so make sure you have a good stock of them.

Though I didn't think to do this, it would have been wise to teach and review how students can help during an emergency. Mainly, they are to remain calm, respectful to the student in need (no laughter or noises of disgust), and wait patiently until you ask for their help. After the emergency, praise the students for the specific ways they helped you. This is a great time to reinforce character traits such as the compassion and helpfulness they demonstrated.

My students were constantly wanting to read parts of their books to me. I was excited to tell my students that they would have a chance to read a book of their choice to fifth-grade students tomorrow during Special Centers. Based on their reactions, many wanted the opportunity to read to a fifth-grade student. I advised them to think of a book they would like to read. In the future, I will give them more time to select a book and practice reading it before the fifth-graders come.

After school, I prepared for the reading aloud activity. With just 30 minutes for the cross-age read aloud, I wanted it to run smoothly and for the 5th-grade students to feel like teachers. So, I labeled colored folders, one for each fifth-grade student, and put them in a box. In each folder. I put ten large-size index cards. On each index card I wrote headings for the students to write their name, the first name of the first-grade student, and the name of the book. The first day of the read-aloud sessions, I showed the older students how to check in when they entered our classroom and how to fill out information on the index card, before they leave.

An uplifting result of the cross-age read aloud sessions is that some of my students told me after the fifth-grade students left, that they had to help the fifth-grade student read some of the words.

Inside the Classroom, April 14

This was the last day of school before Spring Break. We administered the Gates-MacGinitie standardized test to our students. I can readily see where abuses in standardized testing can occur. We proctored our own exams. This should not happen. A proctor should be in the classrooms along with the teacher to ensure that teachers follow the required script for administering the test. During the time all first grades were involved in testing, we were interrupted twice by the intercom.

First grade students do not know how to check for errors. I told the children who finished the test early to go back and check their work. To my horror, I noticed that they were erasing the right answers and marking the wrong answers. I quickly picked up the test booklets when the children were done to stop this carnage. When we return to school, I plan to help students work on test taking strategies.

Teacher-to-Teacher Commentary

Not all teachers at my school knew or followed the rules for giving standardized tests and therefore could not communicate them to their students. For younger students who have not experienced standardized tests, it is essential that they are familiar with the format. Making up your own versions of a test to match the format and types of questions students will find on standardized tests is one way to help relieve anxiety, and in the case of my first-grade students, weariness.

A timed test to my students was to work as fast as possible as they did in the Race the Clock activity described in the September 23 entry. Telling my students to check their answers was a HUGE mistake. Not only did I feel guilty breaking away from the script I was to follow but was horrified when my students began to erase correct answers and marking wrong ones. I should have taught my students how to check for reasonableness long BEFORE giving the test.

The following are just a few other things I would do legally and morally to help my students weeks before the test:

> 1. Have them practice using formats similar to the ones they will encounter on the test.
> 2. Teach the vocabulary commonly used in directions.
> 3. Teach a variety of strategies to use during the test such as following directions, check for reasonable answers, time management, and thinking critically.

Inside the Classroom, April 19

I believe a major cultural difference between my experiences and the experiences my students have grown up with is paddling. Based on parent comments, paddling is the preferred punishment when I send a "bad note" home. The principal, Ms. Wrigley threatens to use the paddle each time she wants the children to conform to her wishes or demands. For instance, the children who ride Mr. Coman's bus are to leave class ten minutes early. Over a lengthy intercom announcement, the principal said that if students who came out were not on Mr. Coman's bus or came out early, she would paddle them. Also, if students who are scheduled to ride the bus did not come out right away, they too would be paddled. I've heard teachers talk about how hard some of them paddle their children, and no one seems upset by this.

Teacher-to-Teacher Commentary

I continuously try to understand some of the root causes of my children's behavioral problems. Today, one little girl mentioned that someone in our class looked drunk. I asked her how she knew someone looked drunk and she said, "My daddy be drunk on Friday nights." Behaviors many children see and experience at home add to the difficulties you will cope with at school. I find it incredibly sad that the students in my school experience physical forms of punishment at home and again at school. It is all they know.

I continued to remain positive, something my children badly needed, by looking into their eyes when I was ready to speak out in anger. This simple strategy helped me remember I am dealing with more than a troublemaker. I am dealing with a little person with needs and wants who does not always live in the most ideal circumstances.

Inside the Classroom, April 21

Julious threatened at least five of the children in my class, who claimed he was going to beat them up after school. He vehemently denied it saying they didn't hear him right. In fact, he said, he was telling the other children he was NOT going to beat them up. Though I called his mother and reported this to Ms. Wrigley, there was no mention of suspension. So far, he gets only warnings and a paddling from the office. It is tragic that Julious with all his good points, and he has many, is being brought down by his behavior.

Teacher-to-Teacher Commentary

Suspend or not to suspend is a difficult problem for school administrators. Suspension, usually reserved for serious or prolonged bad behavior, is a way of giving up on preventative procedures such as threats, warnings, and extra work. Unless the student being suspended has threatened or hurt another child, it is best to consider alternative punishments. From my experience, an alternative is talking with the student and parents, a team approach. However, unless a specialist is involved, there is not a clear idea of how to converse on the student's offenses no matter how heartfelt. The problem is deeper than that. When a student is suspended, the student is rewarded with one or more days off from school. The parents and guardians, most who work, are faced with the inconvenience of staying home and missing work, or leaving a young child, already in trouble for bad behavior, alone. Only one of my students was suspended to protect the students who were afraid to walk home for fear of being attacked. To suspend a student who has hurt or threatened to hurt others, in my opinion, is justified. Alternative treatments for the offending student should be explored and implemented with the understanding that there are no quick fixes.

Inside the Classroom, April 24

We have just returned from Spring Break and even more instructional time has been spoken for. We now have to learn and teach the Hubert Jones Elementary School song. I might think it was a good idea, school spirit and the introduction to some large words would benefit my children. However, Ms. Wrigley said that the teachers and their students had to know the song by Friday and went on to say she would be calling individual classes to the office each day to have them sing the song for her. My lesson was interrupted two more times because of the song. After a lengthy introduction to the song, we were treated to a static-filled rendition over the intercom just as I was getting ready to test my children. The second interruption occurred five minutes before the end of class to remind us of the school song. We had another lengthy harangue followed by another static-filled rendition of the Hubert Jones Elementary School song. I hope they give me the printed words to the song.

All in one day, another intrusion to instructional time occurred. Concessions that were once sold weekly are now sold daily. Assistants and fifth and sixth-grade students knock on my door to sell drinks, candy, and popcorn. I made a rule with my class that they could only bring in money to buy concessions on Friday. Once Ms. Wrigley learned from the assistants that I only allowed my students to buy concessions once a week she came to my room and asked why I was not allowing my students to buy concessions every day. I told her it was disruptive and took too much instructional time away from my class. She told me that the school needs the money from the concession sales and I must let my class participate. I now will allow my children to buy concessions daily, but they have to take them home rather than eat them in class. This will minimize the loss of instructional time and the unhappy faces of the children who do not have money for concessions.

Teacher-to-Teacher Commentary

No matter how efficiently the administrative duties such as attendance and lunch money were done by the teachers, much of the students' time was spent in lines and in transitions. In all, we have about 450 minutes of school time each day (7.5 hours). One hundred and twenty minutes of that time is absorbed by the administrative overhead of running the school. We lose another 30 minutes of every student's instructional time because of specific issues that may not be applicable to every student. So, for each school day's 450 minutes, we lose 150 valuable minutes of instructional time.

Total school day.............................450 minutes
Classroom duties (recess, lunch, roll call) 120 minutes
Unanticipated interruptions............…..........30 minutes
Total possible instructional time.............300 minutes

But wait! Now we come to the critical loss of instructional time, disciplinary issues: Both researchers Hampton (2021) and Cuttler(2019) agree that this loss is about 144 minutes per week. That's about 30 minutes per day. If we subtract the "disciplinary issue" time from the possible instructional time, we get 270 minutes of likely instructional time each day. The numbers are striking: 270 minutes per day of learning is only 60% of the entire school day (450 minutes). Thus, we lose 40% of the school day from all causes. The only part of the loss that the classroom teacher *may* have some control over is small: 30 minutes. But even that, when multiplied over an entire school year of 180 days is 90 hours and is worth trying to save.

Inside the Classroom, April 26

Julious has no remorse or control over his actions toward others. Today, two of my girls were afraid to walk around the playground because he threatened to beat them up. One of my boys said that Julious threatened to beat him up on his way home. After school, I received a phone call from the mother of a little girl telling me that she received harassing phone calls of someone whispering and calling her dirty names. Julious? We don't know. Given Julious's prior misbehavior and threats, the principal talked to him and expelled him for a week. All the prior warnings and expulsion had had no effect. Julious's behavior is just heartbreaking. He is one of my brightest students and has such an engaging personality. He could do so much with his life, but all the signs at this point are very troubling.

Teacher-to-Teacher Commentary

I am still faced with the dilemma of suspension and how to keep my students safe. Julious is the only student in my class who has shown such troubling behavior. His prior expulsion certainly did not change his behavior. Though his mother wanted to help, she too had little to no effect. I looked for reasons for his need to bully others. Without a school specialist, I asked teachers who had previously taught him. Because he had been retained twice, two of them had already dealt with his need to threaten and bully others. Basically, all I heard were complaints, no solutions. They were as lost as I am. I have helped Julious academically, but I feel a profound sense of inadequacy knowing I cannot help him work through his behavior problems.

Inside the Classroom, April 28

I just came across some notes from our RAISE meeting back in October. Several of the notes I had previously written about students in a level one low-performing school continue to be true for my class. Here are two worth considering.

1. Students lack background experiences described in old basal readers making it hard for them to make connections between the positive message from the stories they read and appropriate behavior in their lives. The experiences of the children in the stories of my old set of first-grade readers do not match the ones of my students. My children may have had similar experiences, in varying degrees with pets (most have dogs) and picnics with family and friends. However, a positive father-figure is not present for most students. The majority of my students are being raised by single mothers or grandmothers.

2. Many of my students have experienced violence in their young lives. For example, LaRhonda said that her mother was dead. When Laeticia heard this, she asked who killed her. Jalen told me that a man was stabbed to death in the house where his father lived and his father had to move. De'Andre told me his sister was in jail for trying to kill his mother. Other children calmly and matter-of-factly have told me about their family members going to jail for drugs, robbery, and auto-related offenses. All of these real-life home experiences undoubtedly contributed to the behaviors students exhibit in school. They were unable to relate to the experiences of "Dick and Jane" (Scott Foresman) and "Tom and Betty" (Ginn) that featured an intact white family with a mother and father. The characters and stories in these unrevised popular series did not match the family life and experiences of my children.

Teacher-to-Teacher Commentary

On my drive home, I see children after school playing together in the front yard of a house with mothers sitting on the porch watching them and visiting. This reminds me of a Norman Rockwell scene. However, inside many of these homes, children experience entirely different experiences. Throughout the school year I heard of horrible experiences such as fire, fights, and even death. Though evidence of physical child abuse was evident in my class one time, I can only imagine the neglect, mental abuse, and violent adult behaviors my children were exposed to on a daily basis.

The disturbing behavior of my students reminded me of the earlier statement made by a RAISE presenter in October. Bear with me, it is worth repeating, "We never know what happened to the students the night before they came to us." This certainly applied to the students in my class throughout the school year. For example, one little girl was talking to me while I was distracted gathering homework papers to return to students when she said, "... and one man fell off the roof landed on nails and was dead." It broke through to me that she had just witnessed a terribly traumatizing event, yet I expected her to pay attention to her school work just hours later. Another child told me how she visited her father in jail, another had to flee from a house fire, and on and on it goes for the children.

Inside the Classroom, May 3

Some of my children were disappointing today. They were to write a card to two little girls who were celebrating their "unbirthday." Throughout the year, we celebrated the children's birthdays during the school year by writing individual birthday cards and presenting them to the birthday child. We honored their birthdays by giving them a paper crown and privileges such as line leader and class messenger. For children whose birthdays do not come during the school year, we honor them with an unbirthday party complete with birthday cards, a crown, and special privileges in the days before school ended. Today, Delon's card caused a lot of commotion with a picture of him going to the bathroom showing the correct anatomical part! Though many of the other cards were sweet and well written, others were hastily and carelessly made. My little unbirthday children were receiving the brunt of a class tired of making cards. Next year I think I will sprinkle the unbirthdays throughout the school year. I am looking forward to a second year because I have learned so much about my students and the things that worked and the things that didn't. I have already started thinking about ways I could better help my students learn.

Teacher-to-Teacher Commentary

My intention of returning to my school for a second year was never realized. An unexpected offer of a coveted job in the School of Education at the University of Mississippi was hard to turn down. My original intent was to return to teaching at an elementary school to become a better professor for my university students studying to become teachers. However, the decision to leave my school and the children I taught was fraught with sleepless nights. I had been excited to apply all I learned this year to my next class of elementary students.

Inside the Classroom, May 8

As the end of school nears, the pacing of the lessons has become more difficult. There is so much I want my students to learn. I scaled down what I felt I could directly teach effectively and worked on many active and hands-on activities to let the children move. Focusing and refocusing the children's attention takes a large chunk of my instructional time. I get the feeling that the students and the teachers are beginning to let down with a little over two weeks of school left.

I worry about today's students who, like Julious, were off to a rough start with little behavioral improvement. Teachers have told me that behavior problems in school have become even worse. Common events, even for young students, have escalated to the destruction of property, physical attacks on one another, stealing, and disregard for personal rights and property. Couple this rise in illegal behaviors with social media and peer pressure. Teachers, parents, and caregivers have their hands full.

Teacher-to-Teacher Commentary

With the end of school on their minds, it becomes harder to get and keep students' attention on their work. The spring weather and the anticipation of summer vacation contributes to an unease or excitement experienced by both teachers and students. With testing over and grades likely submitted, students no longer have two of the pressures that prompted them to work. They begin to let down in their behavior and in their schoolwork.

There are so many basic skills I want my students to take with them as they advance to the next grade. I have noticed the letdown occurs with students of all ages whether they are in first grade or college.

As a professional, push aside your own yearnings for the freedom you are eager to embrace. It is your duty to continue to teach until the last child leaves your classroom. Capitalize on the days and hours you have left. Continue to talk to offending students with poor behavior or poor academic performance and set daily goals all the way to the end of school.

To bolster your students' confidence, involve them in end-of-school activities that showcase all the work they have done and all they have learned. You can celebrate their accomplishments by helping them make lists of the important things they learned and hang them on the bulletin board or post them on a large chart.

If you gave your students daily goals throughout the year and you saved them, put them together into a little booklet for students to keep as a reminder of their hard work and accomplishments. To represent their hard work throughout the year, show them how to make a collage from their art and written work that represents the high points they had throughout the year.

Inside the Classroom, May 12

Julious was suspended and I was the last to know. After prank calls and threats to beat up other children in my class, I was told by Ms. Wrigley that Julious would be suspended. I was for suspension because he had become such a threat to so many of my children. However, until today he continued to come to my class. Friday, the children in my class told me that Julious was suspended. No parent conference, and certainly no notification to me, his teacher.

Teacher-to-Teacher Commentary

A government website offers practical advice for teachers who are struggling to control bullying in class: (https://www.stopbullying.gov/prevention/at-school). What I liked about this website is that it gave very practical advice on the steps to take to prevent bullying. To stop bullying, they suggest that suspicions or documented evidence of bullying must first be addressed by the teacher and shared with the school counselor. The next steps are to involve the principal, superintendent, and ultimately the state department of education. At each step of the ladder, people who have the power and the resources to implement antibullying programs become involved. Meanwhile, at the first sign of malicious behavior toward others, the teacher should contact the parents and caregivers. This initial step may have been absent from the government website list because they wanted teachers to gather information about school policies to have a substantive conversation.

Inside the Classroom, May 15

Our grades had to be turned in and recorded in the cumulative files today. This was two weeks before school ended. I suspect many teachers have seriously quit teaching after their grades were turned in and after the standardized testing. I have seen them take their students outside, show movies, or have them help clean the room. When I walk by almost any classroom, the teachers are packing and cleaning rather than teaching. Even the parents have slacked off; my attendance this week has been way down. Usually, I have had perfect or near perfect attendance. During the school year I had been proud of this. I have been told by many mothers that their children want to come to school, another one of those rare, yet badly needed, positive strokes. However, on Monday I had six absent, on Tuesday I had seven.

Teacher-to-Teacher Commentary

Nothing sets me off more than seeing and learning of the way many teachers stop teaching after standardized tests are given. They have taught to the test rather than focusing on student learning. What other profession pays its workers for not working? By now, you have seen my emphasis on the importance of maximizing instructional time that has led to my observations and shock when teachers do not use every minute of the time they have to teach.

Sadly, one way I noticed wasted teaching and learning time is that teachers give lots of seat work and then sit at their desks, some drinking coffee and others on their phones. I observed this problem in multiple districts over several years in schools who serve students from all economic levels.

The last day of school is Friday, May 26, a half day. Teachers still have 9.5 days, 71.5 hours to teach. This is a lot of valuable instructional time to squander away.

Inside the Classroom, May 19

Memories of a positive approach to discipline that I used in a third-grade class in Virginia guided me throughout the school year with my first-grade class (see entry for August 23). When I stumbled and reverted to a negative approach such as an angry voice and threats, the behavior of my students though initially subdued, became noticeably worse. A teacher's positive attitude goes a long way to create a happy environment for learning.

Our large stuffed dog, Buddy, who sits in front of the class waiting to help a child in need or reward students for good behavior continued to be a hit throughout the year. My students never outgrew the need to hold him in their laps. It is fun to picture my oldest and toughest boys sitting like a little child with a stuffed animal in their lap. The children were allowed to hold the dog for as long as they wanted before returning it to the chair in the front of the classroom. Though there were multiple opportunities for misbehavior such as hoarding the dog, throwing the dog, making barking noises, and taking a long way around the classroom to return the dog to the chair, my children never abused the privilege of holding Buddy.

Teacher-to-Teacher Commentary

Stillman (2018) cites a study by Chen, L. et al (2018) on 240 students ages 7-10 about the way attitude affects their mathematics performance. By studying images of their brains, she found that the part of the brain, the hippocampus, responsible for learning and memory was activated through positive thinking. I think you will find this quote from Chen's article on attitude interesting: "A good attitude opens the door to high achievement, which means you then have a better attitude getting you into a good circle of learning." Taking it a step further, a poor attitude can go the other way and become a vicious circle of hopelessness. This means that we must think of ways to engage our students in positive thinking. The following are a collection of easy-to-use ways I have used to help my students develop a positive attitude:

1. Set reasonable goals your students can meet and then celebrate meeting them.
2. Build students' ideas into your lessons and give credit by mentioning their names.

3. Have students show you their best work by letting them mark it with a star or other symbol. If they incorrectly marked the wrong one, point out the one you think is their best work and discuss why. Give students an opportunity to re-mark their best work. My students loved to draw a little star over their best work.

4. Personalize praise by quietly praising your students individually to avoid embarrassment and interrupting the rest of the class.

5. Save your students' work in a portfolio to show the progression of learning. The portfolio can be as simple as a manilla folder where you date and store selected pieces of work in chronological order. See the March 9 entry for *Inside the Classroom,* for a comment from a student that brought tears to my eyes.

I personally found that my attitude affected my performance. I found that positive thinking had a strong impact on my attitude and work habits. Try it and see if it works for you! When you approach working on a project, think to yourself that today you will do your best work ever! If you are like me, you can even go further by thinking that you will come up with a wonderful or unique idea to use in your work. The "I think I can" attitude from the book, *The Little Engine That Could,* is a good example of positive thinking and perseverance that applies to people of all ages.

Inside the Classroom, May 22

The last week of school. There are new interruptions that take away time from instructional time and learning. An hour before dismissal, students from the fifth and sixth grade come to sweep the room or empty our trash cans. My children know most of the children who come into our room so they stop paying attention to the lesson and want to say hello to and talk to them.

Many teachers have not taught for over a week. My attendance this week continues to be down by six or seven children each day. I have heard that teachers are telling their students not to come to school. Several times I have heard teachers in the hallway angrily ask their students why they were at school. Imagine, students were getting in trouble for coming to school! What an appalling message to students that they are unwelcome in their own classroom!!

Teacher-to-Teacher Commentary

This coming Friday is the last day of school. Today is only Monday. Teachers still have 33.5 hours to teach. This is a lot of valuable instructional time to squander away. By now, you have read my emphasis on the importance of maximizing instructional time. I hope you are not tired of it and take it as seriously as I do. Why do teachers who have one of the most important jobs, helping children prepare for a successful future, feel they can take the last few days and final hours off?

Inside the Classroom, May 25

Yesterday, after school I displayed all the games, puzzles, and manipulatives in the front of the classroom from the Special Centers. This morning, I had my children write me a note telling me which one they would like to have and describe why they wanted it. With fewer children attending class, I had no problems giving them the ones they wanted based on their written preferences. They left class with their back-packs bulging.

Interruptions to our instructional time had become worse. Fifth and sixth grade students continue to leave their classrooms to empty garbage and sweep the other classrooms. Ms. Wrigley has pulled students from all grades to help her clean the cafeteria. Thankfully, this has only happened to my class once.

Teacher-to-Teacher Commentary

Keeping the students' attitude positive by planning real-life ways to approach learning is certainly important. My children used their writing skills to write me a note telling me which of the games, puzzles, and manipulatives they would like to take home. This involved critical thinking and persuasive writing. As usual, the frequent interruptions disturbed the flow of their writing. If I had given out these materials a day earlier, I could have had my students brainstorm ideas they wanted to include in their thank you notes and even written a little draft. However, this was a meaningful and authentic writing opportunity that is worth doing again.

Administrative interruptions that come out of the blue after the early morning Pledge of Allegiance, patriotic song, and initial school-wide announcements should be kept to a minimum. Interruptions blasted school-wide during instructional time should be for safety and for schedule changes. Certainly, administrators and teachers could work together to take steps to solve the interruption problem.

Inside the Classroom, May 26

This is the last day of school. It should be a happy one for students, but unfortunately, again they were being questioned by teachers about why they came to school. When I arrived at school for my 7:05 duty I saw at least two angry teachers who had told their students not to come today. I heard these teachers angrily ask why they came. Again, I couldn't believe my ears! This was a school day. Out of 20 children, I had 12 children come, the highest attendance of the teachers I talked to. Some teachers only had two students. Such a waste of instructional time!

This was a sad day for me because I was losing my children. Because I would be teaching at the university next year, I knew I would not see them again except for brief returns to the school. The classes were dismissed so suddenly that neither the children nor I had time to reflect on the finality of the moment. We were told this was to be a 60% day which meant that the children would leave between 12:00-1:00. I had planned some fun learning experiences for my children and wanted to give out books from our classroom library to read over the summer. I was called over the intercom to dismiss my students at 11:20! I was not prepared. My children had little time to select the books they wanted and stuff them in their backpacks. They were so excited and told me they were going to read the books to their parents and grandparents. Some of my children wrote me cute notes and many told me they didn't want school to end. Leaving them is hard!

Teacher-to-Teacher Commentary

Because students' behavior is critically important to learning, behavior had become a reoccurring theme beginning from the first day of school and continuing to the end of school. For a classroom to run smoothly with little wasted instructional time, you will be called upon to be proficient at many things. You must become experts on the topics of the lessons you teach, the use of technology, the needs of your students, and clearly articulated behavioral rules and consequences. Through experience, I have learned that all of this preparation is necessary to maximize the precious limited instructional time you have for each lesson. Recent research by Anderson (2023) about preparedness and organization supports what I learned the hard way.

It is vital to recognize that discipline is the sine qua non for learning. Throughout the year, I was constantly reminded of the toll behavioral disruptions took on learning. The time I spent on interruptions and discipline was time NOT spent on teaching and learning. Hampton (2021) and Cuttler (2019) found this added up to three full weeks of school. Going back to a famous question, "What comes first, the chicken or the egg?" can be rewritten to ask, "What comes first, behavior management or academic instruction?" The answer is up to the teachers.

The following quote sums up my feelings about teaching, "Even though I love my job and work harder at it than I've ever worked for anything, the loudest voice in my head is the one that is constantly saying *you're not doing enough.*" *(unknown 5th grade teacher).*

Joy and Heartbreak

Epilogue

Five Years Later

When I returned for a visit, I learned that my five students who had been socially skip promoted plus three from the other first-grade classes had been pulled an hour a day from their third-grade classes and were being tutored in reading by an assistant teacher who said they were "doin' real good."

Julious, the child who liked to sit and flex his muscles, and created problems in the bathroom and playground, is in the school choir and doing well. He is well-liked by his teachers, yet surprisingly, struggling academically.

Tragically De'Andre has not fared as well. He had far too many strikes against him including teachers who were put off by his physical appearance and rowdy behavior. His behavioral problems are still legendary. Though he was on the honor roll in my class, he is not doing well academically.

Jaden, my shy child who struggled academically all year in my classroom, was finally ruled eligible for special education services. Despite my wishes, he was promoted to the second grade. I have heard that he is still struggling in school. Perhaps it is best that he is at least with his age-mates.

LeTorr has moved out of the district, so I will never know the effects social promotion had on his school performance. He did not exhibit the same level of disruptive behavior as De'Andre and Julious. However, the three of them were easily distracted, moved constantly in their seats, and were frequently off task. Despite their restless behavior, they excelled in reading and math in my class. They were somewhat taller than the average first-grade student and boyishly slender. They had been retained twice. I hope they are doing well!

The five boys who had been skip promoted were a part of a group of nine children in my class who had been held back the previous year because of their poor academic progress in reading, language arts, and mathematics. I remember clearly my sense of disbelief and frustration when I was told that these five students would be socially skip promoted to the third grade, missing second-grade altogether. I had no idea about the existing controversy on social promotion and how it grew to become a hot topic when the accountability measures from the 2001 No Child left Behind Act were implemented. Protected by the cocoon of my classroom, I only had a very narrow glimpse of a much larger picture. My world centered around the five little boys who were targeted by the principal for a social skip promotion because of prior repeated retentions that made them the oldest students in my class. De'Andre, Antonio, Julious, Tyrus, and Jaden. Though appalled at the idea of any of my children skipping a grade, my fears were greatest for these children, each for a different reason.

Jaden, unlike De'Andre, usually had a very quiet disposition. He looked up at me through long eye lashes and was slow to smile. He had failed kindergarten and first grade and at age nine was repeating first grade. He was stocky and about the same size as the taller traditional first grade students. I met with his mother and gave her some books and math manipulatives to use with him at home. However, I held out little hope he would receive this extra attention because his mother had tried to convince me that her son was slow and incapable of learning. He was not making much progress in my class and I tried for a good part of the second semester to have him evaluated for special education services. With Jaden's shy nature and his continuous struggle to learn academic skills, I feared he would be crushed by another year of academic hardship resulting from being skip promoted.

De'Andre, the child you have met several times through my journal, was a skinny child with knock-knees, a twinkle in his eye, and a face shiny from drool. He already had experienced failure, having repeated preschool, kindergarten, and first grade before he came to my class. His behavior was legendary, serious enough for me to request a psychological evaluation. He came to school each day happy and kept the class in good spirits with his quick thinking and antics. In my mind, experiencing failure by missing a grade, could only lead to worse problems.

Julious though exhibiting behaviors serious enough for suspension, I thought stood a good chance of "making it" in the third grade. He was the largest, most physically developed of the group. He was the one who one who liked to show off his arm muscles and looked like an athlete. His social skills were outstanding. He was such a charmer with his quick smile and large brown eyes, yet he was sexually precocious, generally rambunctious, and threatening to many of the younger children. He had experienced two years of failure, once in kindergarten and the other in first grade. He loved to write and work arithmetic problems.

Except for Jaden, the students targeted for skip promotion were a boisterous lot. I was sure skipping my students over a grade would take away the confidence they were building from their improved academic success, leaving them with even more behavioral problems to fill the void. I believe that behavior, not innate intelligence was at the root of the academic problems. The one thing all my children who had previously been retained had in common was their fear of failing.

I had two little girls in my class with the same name, Angelina, who were as different as night and day. One Angelina talked and complained a lot. Her work was average, mainly because she did not pay attention to the lessons. The other Angelina was a model student who was enrolled in my class during the second semester. She loved to read and brought in books with Bible verses and read them every chance she got. Apparently, I worried about the wrong Angelina. I was told by Ms. Miller, that the Angelina who complained and did not focus on her lesson was doing very well in school. The "good" Angelina turned out to be a trouble maker and was not living up to her potential as I saw

Joy and Heartbreak

it. I heard that there were family problems that most likely had a profound effect on her behavior and learning.

During the time she was a first-grade teacher, my mentor, Ms. Miller became a National Board-Certified Teacher. To have earned the prestigious certification, Ms. Miller clearly demonstrated the traits throughout our time together that fulfilled the following Five Core Propositions for exceptional teaching:

1: Teachers are committed to students and their learning
2: Teachers know the subjects they teach and how to teach those subjects to students
3: Teachers are responsible for managing and monitoring student learning
4: Teachers think systematically about their practice and learn from experience
5: Teachers are members of a learning community

Ms. Wrigley, my principal, was replaced by a well-respected teacher the following year. I was told that the teachers now send their students to computer class, art, class, and the library which gave them much-needed breaks. The unintended consequences were that the conscientious teachers complained their day was too chopped up and they had to shorten their lessons to accommodate the breaks.

My assistant is still at the school despite her intense dislike of the students. I saw her in the hallway and she turned away and ignored me. I was told she rotated among the teachers. I assume that no one teacher wanted her full time, but that is just an assumption on my part.

Challenges to Learning During the 2020-2021 Covid Pandemic

The dramatic change from the traditional face-to-face learning in the classroom to online learning at home occurred when schools closed due to Covid. Almost overnight, states and districts had to come up with ways to teach their students at home. Some required students to receive all online instruction while others allowed a hybrid or blended system of online and in-class education. When they were in the classroom, all students would have access to the online sources that many may not have access to at home.

For a good source of information on the use of blended learning, we recommend an article published by the Association for Supervision and Curriculum Development (ASCD) by Juliana Finegan (2017).

During the height of Covid in the years 2020-2021, students spent the school day at home communicating with their teacher and classmates through online classroom meetings. Programs such as Schoology were used for the younger students while Zoom and Seesaw were used for the older students. Text chat enabled students to talk with one another but could be blocked by the teacher if students were off task or for crude language. Sitting comfortably in a chair, students could go on virtual field trips, engage in interactive virtual reality, see live pictures of events in the solar system, and explore microscopic views of plants and animals. An excellent source of online instruction for students of all ages is through the Khan Academy (2024). Khan Academy offers a series of free short lessons on a variety of topics including mathematics, science, and history.

Now, in 2023-2025, the students are back to school and, depending on the state and country, wearing masks is not mandatory. So, everything is good, right? Wrong, students who for too long were isolated from their peers, began to misbehave. Teachers knew it would be difficult for students to adjust to returning to school after almost a year away, but they weren't prepared to deal with the social-emotional trauma the students had experienced due to isolation. Academic recovery is one thing, classroom behavior is another. Students who had been isolated at home have to relearn social interactions and the numerous behaviors that lead to learning (Williams, 2023).

The upheaval in American education resulted in a significant drop in the 2022 reading and math test scores reported by the National Association of Educational Progress.

The Mississippi Miracle

The Nations Report Card (NAEP, 2022) a government organization and website that displays the results of reading and mathematics test scores for the entire nation has noted that reading scores have been declining since 2017. Of course, a major part of the decline in 2022 was likely caused by the pandemic. Nationwide, scores showed the largest decline in 30 years.

What happened to recent Mississippi reading scores? They rose from being 46th in 2017 to 22nd in the nation in 2022. Called the "Mississippi Miracle," there has been a sustained effort on the part of the Mississippi State Department of Education (MDE) to improve reading scores. This miracle took place due to the efforts of education leaders and teachers. Beginning in 2014, more than fifteen thousand Mississippi teachers have undergone training in the science of reading through the LETRS (Language Essentials for Teachers of Reading and Spelling) program in multiple workshops. At the same time, the MDE required that phonics courses were to be developed and taught in all Mississippi public universities. Although this was resisted by some university Schools of Education reading faculty, enough of the substance found its way into the classroom. The headline of an article by Emily Hanford (2019) for the New York Times sums up the reasons for Mississippi's success that began in 2015 and continued in 2022. "There is a science to teaching reading and Mississippi knows it."

References

Ackerman, C. (2017). *40 empathy activities and worksheets for students and adults.* https://positivepsychology.com/kindness-activities-empathy-worksheets/#teach-kindness

Anderson, J. (2023). *Why organization Is important for teachers.* The highly effective teacher.com https://thehighlyeffectiveteacher.com/why-organization-is-important-for-teachers/

Basit, A., Martig, J., Dietzel, M. Constable, P., Jacobs, M. (2023). *The science of word recognition.* Microsoft. https://learn.microsoft.com/en-us/typography/develop/word-recognition

Berwick, C. (2019). *What does the research say about testing?* Eutopia. https://www.edutopia.org/article/what-does-research-say-about-testing?fbclid=IwAR28O5Hhcz0flBErdoir19uyBiumHyD4c1tsmw_pKhf_gcvvsAMXMpGri2Y

Campbell University Wiggins Memorial Library (2022). *Learning through inquiry: Makerspaces, manipulatives, and board games.* https://guides.lib.campbell.edu/c.php?g=325978&p=2667668

Character Kid Lit (n.d.) *Children's books that inspire awe and wonder.* https://characterkidlit.com/blog/picture-books-that-inspire-awe-and-wonder

Chen, L., Battista, C., Quin, S., Chen, T., Evans, V.M. (2018). *Positive attitude toward math supports early academic success: Behavioral evidence and neurocognitive mechanisms.* Psychological Science. https://www.sciencedaily.com/releases/2018/01/180124131736.html

Chu, L. (2017). *Little soldiers: An American boy in a Chinese school, and the global race to achieve.* Harper.

Common Core State Standards Initiative (2021). https://www.thecorestandards.org/Math/

Cooper, H., Robinson, J.C. & Patall, E.A. (2006). *Does homework improve academic achievement? A synthesis of research, 1982-2003.* Review of Educational Research 76 (1). https://assess.ucr.edu/sites/default/files/2019-02/cooperrobinsonpatall_2006.pdf

Cox, T. (November 21, 2023). *300 most common English words (and how to learn them fast)* Preply blog. https://preply.com/en/blog/300-most-common-english-words/

Cuttler, G. (2019). *Educators report growing behavioral issues among young students*. EAB Global Newswire. https://www.globenewswire.com/news-release/2019/02/14/1725406/0/en/Educators-Report-Growing-Behavioral-Issues-Among-Young-Students.html

Dewey, J. (1971). *The child and curriculum: The school and society*. The University of Chicago Press. Chicago, IL.

Dilberti, M.K., H.L. Schwartz, & D. Grant, (2021). *Stress topped the reasons why public school teachers quit, even before Covid-19*. Rand Corporation. https://www.rand.org/content/dam/rand/pubs/research_reports/RRA1100/RRA1121-2/RAND_RRA1121-2.pdf

Drew, C. (2023). *27 Top Homework pros and cons*. Helpful Professor.com https://helpfulprofessor.com/pros-and-cons-of-homework/

Duffin, E. (2023). *Pre-primary school enrollment (kindergarten, nursery) for children aged 3-5 years from 1970-2021)*. Statista: Society, Education, and Science. https://www.statista.com/statistics/184020/kindergarten-enrollment-in-public-and-private-institutions/

Edmentum (Oct. 19, 2023,). *Mississippi Delta teacher shortage*. https://blog.edmentum.com/addressing-teacher-shortage-mississippi

Esquith, R. (2003). *There are no shortcuts*. Anchor Books.

Esquith, R. (2007). *Teach like your hair's on fire.* Penguin Group.

Finegan, J. (2017). *Solving the problem of teaching to the middle.* Association for Supervision and Curriculum Development (ASCD). https://www.ascd.org/el/articles/solving-the-problem-of-teaching-to-the-middle

Foster, C.B. (2020). *Cooperative learning and how to use it in the classroom.* TeachHUB https://www.teachhub.com/teaching-strategies/2020/07/cooperative-learning-and-how-to-use-it-in-the-classroom/

Freyer, R.G. (2011). *Financial incentives and student achievement: Evidence from randomized trials.* https://scholar.harvard.edu/sites/scholar.harvard.edu/files/fryer/files/financial_incentives_and_student_achievement_evidence_from_randomized_trials.pdf

Ginott, H.G. (2003). *Between parent and child: Revised and updated.* Harmony/Rodale

Ginott, H. G. (1972) *Between teacher and child.* The Macmillan Company.

Good, T.L. & Brophy, J.E. *Looking in Classrooms,* 9th edition. Allyn & Bacon.

Grande, D. (2020, June, 2). *Active listening skills: Why active listening is important and how to do it.* Psychology Today. https://www.psychologytoday.com/us/blog/in-it-together/202006/active-listening-skills

Hale, J.M. (1986). *Black children: Their roots, culture, and learning styles.* Johns Hopkins University Press.

Hall, M. S. & Burns, M. B. (2017). *Meta-analysis of targeted small group reading interventions.* Journal of School Psychology 66. https://www.researchgate.net/publication/321116132_Meta-analysis_of_targeted_small-group_reading_interventions

Hampton, L. (2021). *Behavior management in the classroom or academic instruction: What comes first?* LEARNING-FOCUSED https://learningfocused.com/behavior-management-or-academic-instruction-what-comes-first/

Hanford, E. (2019) *"There Is a Right Way to Teach Reading and Mississippi Knows It:" The state's reliance on cognitive science explains why."* New York Times. https://www.nytimes.com/2019/12/05/opinion/mississippi-schools-naep.html

Hart, B. & Risley, T.R. (1995). *Meaningful differences in the everyday experience of young American children.* Paul H. Brookes Publishing.

Heward, L., Kimbell, J.W., Hechaman, K.A., Dunne, J.D. et al. (2021). *In his own words: Siegfried, "Zig" Engelmann talks about what's wrong with education and how to fix it.* Behavior Analysis Practice 14, pp.766-774. https://doi.org/10.1007/s40617-021-00636-x

Holmes, K. P., Moore, JJ, & Holmes, S.V. (2023). *A sensory approach to STEAM teaching and learning: Materials-based units for students K-6.* Routledge.

Hunter, M. (1982). *Mastery teaching.* TIP Publications. https://w3.gilmerisd.org/w3/Docs/TeacherREs12_The_Lesson_Cycle_Explanation.pdf

Jilani, Z. (2022). *Experiment: Pay students to tackle learning loss.* NEWSNATION https://www.newsnationnow.com/us-news/education/experiment-pay-students-to-tackle-learning-loss/

Johnson, D. W. & Johnson, R. T. (2018) *Cooperative learning: The foundation for active learning.* SEMANTICSCHOLAR https://pdfs.semanticscholar.org/567a/6681bd36e9186018586499925ad576aa7cd1.pdf

Johnson, S. (2023). *A grammar of the English tongue.* Independently published.

Johnston, F.R. (2000) *Word learning in predictable text*. Journal of Educational Psychology, 92, 248-255. American Psychological Association. https://libres.uncg.edu/ir/uncg/f/F_Johnston_Word_2000.pdf

Kennedy-Moore (2018). *Want your child to listen and learn? Don't lecture.* Psychology Today. https://www.psychologytoday.com/us/blog/growing-friendships/201809/want-your-child-listen-and-learn-don-t-lecture

Khan Academy (2024). https://www.khanacademy.org

King, L. H. (1993). *High and low achievers' perceptions and cooperative learning in two small groups.* The Elementary School Journal, 93 (4) pp 399-416.

Kraft, M. and Novicoff, S. (2022). *Instructional time in U.S. public schools- Wide variation, causal effects, and lost hours.* (EdWorkingPaper: 22-653). Annenberg Institute at Brown University: https://doi.org/10.26300/1xxp-9c79

Lama, S.C. (2019). *Licking and vitamin deficiencies in children.* Livestrong.com https://www.livestrong.com/article/475773-licking-vitamin-deficiencies-in-children

Lambert, D. (2022). *Covid challenges, bad student behavior push teachers to limit, out the door.* Edsource. https://edsource.org/2022/covid-challenges-bad-student-behavior-push-teachers-to-the-limit-and-out-the-door/673124

Li, G., Li, Z, Wu, X, & Zhen, R. (2022). *Relations between class competition and primary school students' achievement: Learning anxiety and learning engagement as mediators.* https://www.frontiersin.org/articles/10.3389/fpsyg.2022.775213/full

Mayo Clinic (2021). *Stress relief from laughter? It's no joke.* https://www.mayoclinic.org/healthy-lifestyle/stress-management/in-depth/stress-relief/art-20044456

Minero, E. (2017). *When students are traumatized, teachers are too.* Eutopia https://www.edutopia.org/article/when-students-are-traumatized-teachers-are-too

Mississippi Department of Child Protective Services (2024). https://www.mdcps.ms.gov/

Mississippi Department of Education (2023). *Literacy-Based Promotion Act.* https://www.mdek12.org/OEER/LBPA

Mississippi Department of Education (2022). *Mississippi high school graduation rate highest ever at 88.4%; Dropout rate falls to 8.5%.* https://www.mdek12.org/news/2024/1/18/Mississippis-2022-23-graduation-rate-of-89.4-marks-all-time-high-dropout-rate-falls-to-8.5

Mississippi Updated College and Career-Readiness Standards (2016). https://www.mdek12.org/OAE/college-and-career-readiness-standards

National Association of Education Progress (NAEP, 2022). *Long-term trend assessment results for reading and mathematics.* https://www.nagb.gov/naep-subject-areas/long-term-trend/2022-NAEP-Long-Term-Trend-Release.html

National Association of Education Progress (NAEP, 2022). *Reading and mathematics scores decline during Covid-19 pandemic.* https://www.nationsreportcard.gov/highlights/ltt/2022/

National Core Art Standards (2023). https://www.nationalartsstandards.org/

National Council of Teachers of Mathematics (2000). www.nctm.org

National Institute of Direct Instruction (2024). *Beginnings.* https://www.nifdi.org/research/history-of-di-research/beginnings

Nation's Report Card (2022). *State performance compared to the nation: Reading Grade 4 Data table.* National Assessment of Educational Progress. https://www.nationsreportcard.gov/profiles/statepro file?chort=1&sub=MAT&sj=AL&sfj=NP&st=MN &year=2022R3

Sites at Penn State (2019). *The price of standardized testing.* https://sites.psu.edu/tota19edu/2019/02/07/the-price-of-standardized-testing/

Perry-Jenkins(2023). *How parent's experiences at work impacts their kids.* https://hbr.org/2023/01/how-a-parents-experience-at-work-impacts-their-kids

ProCon, (2023). *Corporal punishment in K-12 schools-Top 3 pros and cons* https://www.procon.org/headlines/corporal-punishment-pros-cons-procon-org/

Random Acts of Kindness Foundation (2024). *Make kindness the norm at your school.* https://www.randomactsofkindness.org/kindergarten-grade-5-lesson-plans

Shanahan, T. (2024). *Should we build a word wall or not?* Reading Rockets https://www.readingrockets.org/blogs/shanahan-on-literacy/should-we-build-word-wall- or-not

Skinner, B. F. (1963). *Operant behavior.* American psychologist, 18 (8), 503. Positive Reinforcement: What Is It and How Does It Work? (simplypsychology.org)

Slavin, R. E. (1985) *Cooperative learning: applying contact theory in desegregated schools.* Journal of Social Issues, 41(3), pp. 45-62.
https://www.edutopia.org/article/when-students-are-traumatized-teachers-are-too

Smolleck, L.A. & Duffy, C.G. (2017). *The role of negative behavior on children's academic performance in early childhood education*
https://www.riverapublications.com/article/the-role-of-negative-behavior-on-childrens-academic-performance-in-early-childhood-education

Spalding, R.B. & Spalding, W.T. (1990). *The writing road to reading: The Spalding method of phonics for teaching, speech, writing, and reading.* Quill, William Morrow.

Sparks, S. D. (2022). *Classroom reading groups: 5 lessons from recent studies.* Education Week.
https://www.edweek.org/teaching-learning/classroom-reading-groups-5-lessons-from-recent-studies/2022/03

Stanovich, K.E. (2000). *Progress in understanding reading: Scientific foundations and new frontiers.* The Guilford Press. New York

Stillman, J. (2018). New Stanford study: *A positive attitude literally makes your brain work better.* INC.
https://www.inc.com/jessica-stillman/stanford-research-attitude-matters-as- much-as-iq-in-kids-success.html

Terada, Y. (2015, July, 31). *Research trends: Why homework should be balanced.* Edutopia. https://www.edutopia.org/blog/research-trends-is-homework-effective-youki-terada

Terada, Y. (2021). *How novice and expert teachers approach classroom management differently.* George Lucas Educational Foundation https://www.edutopia.org/article/how-novice-and-expert-teachers-approach-classroom-management-differently

Torpey, E. (2018). *Projections for teachers: How many are leaving the occupation. U.S.*

Bureau of Labor Statistics. https://www.bls.gov/careeroutlook/2018/data-on-display/how-many-teachers-are-leaving.htm

Trelease, J. & Giorgis, C. (2019). *Jim Trelease's Read-aloud handbook*: Eighth edition. Penguin Books.

University of the People (2023, December, 7). *The pros and cons of homework.* https://www.uopeople.edu/blog/the-pros-and-cons-of-homework/)

Waugaman, E.R. (2015, March, 1). *Our evolving Black American naming traditions: Given names can provide important social and spiritual insights.* Psychology Today. https://www.psychologytoday.com/us/blog/whats-in-name/201503/our-evolving-black-american-naming-traditions

Williams, C.P. (2023). *Covid changed student behavior-How are schools responding?* https://www.edutopia.org/article/covid-changed-student-behavior-how-are-schools- responding

Wilson, D. & Conyers, M. (2017). *4 proven strategies for teaching empathy.* Edutopia https://www.edutopia.org/article/4-proven-strategies-teaching-empathy-donna-wilson-marcus-conyers

Wright, J. (2015). *Analyzing student behavior: A step-by-step guide.* Social-Emotional Behavioral RTI Series. https://www.interventioncentral.org/

Wright, J. (2015). *How to conduct a task analysis and create a behavior checklist.*

Social-Emotional/Behavioral RTI' Series. https://www.interventioncentral.org/sites/default/files/workshop_files/NASP_2016/task_analysis.pdf

Zike, D. (2005). *Classroom organization: It can be done, K-6.* Dinah-Might Adventures, LP

A Sample of Children's Books

Kindness and Feelings
Beautiful Joe by M. Saunders
The Kindness Quilt by N.E. Wallace
Have You Filled a Bucket Today? by C. McCloud
The Foot Book by Dr. Seuss
When the Sky Glows by N. C. Beckerman
Alexander and the Terrible, Horrible, No Good, Very Bad Day by J. Vorst

Black Role Models
Black Boy, Black Boy by Ali Kamanda and Jorge Redmond
Black Heroes of the American Revolution by B. Davis
Great Black Heroes: Five Brave Explorers by W. Hudson and R. Garnett
Great Black Heroes: Five Brilliant Scientists by L. Jones and R. Garnett
I Am Harriet Tubman by Brad Meltzer
I Am Jackie Robinson by Brad Meltzer
Rosa by Nikki Giovanni
The Story of Martin Luther King Jr.: A Biography Book for New Readers by C. Platt
What Will I Be? by Jayla Joseph

Behavior
Charlie and the Chocolate Factory by R. Dahl
Decibella and Her 6 Inch Voice by J. Cook
Don't Tell Suzie No by Belinda Adams
Lacey Walker, Nonstop Talker by C. Jones
The Gingerbread Boy by P. Galdone
When Bobbie Gets Angry by Belinda Adams

Predictable Repetitive Text
Brown Bear, Brown Bear What Do You See? by B. Martin and E. Carle
Is Your Mama a Llama? by Deborah Guarino
Panda Bear, Panda Bear, What Do You See? by B. Martin and E. Carle
Polar Bear, Polar Bear, What Do You See? by B. Martin and E. Carle
There Was an Old Lady who Swallowed a Fly, traditional folk story by Simms Taback

About the Authors

Kerry P. Holmes

Kerry P. Holmes, Ed.D., is a Professor Emerita of Elementary Education at the University of Mississippi. She was awarded The School of Education Outstanding Researcher and Outstanding Faculty Researcher. She taught kindergarten and 1st grade for five years in California, was a substitute teacher in special needs and K-12 classes in Virginia, before teaching 1st grade in a critical-needs school in Mississippi. Her interests include writing original stories with children, piano, and reading historical fiction. Please contact her at kholmes@olemiss.edu

Stacy V. Holmes

Stacy V. Holmes, Ph.D., is Assistant Dean Emeritus, School of Engineering at the University of Mississippi. He spent 27 years in the Navy and retired as a Captain, USN. He began his academic career at the University of Mississippi where he taught electrical engineering and mathematics courses as well as graduate courses in statistics in the School of Education for K-12 teachers. His interests also include sports statistics. He served as the official scorer for the University of Mississippi football games for 27 years. Contact: adholmes@olemiss.edu

Jerilou J. Moore

Jerilou J. Moore, Ph.D., Professor Emerita at the University of Mississippi School of Education, has taught arts for teachers. She enjoyed showing preservice and inservice teachers how to integrate the arts to aid children's physical and social emotional development and enhance learning through creative thinking and problem solving. She was twice awarded Teacher of the Year by students and faculty at the University of Mississippi School of Education. She taught 1st grade for thirteen years, was an elementary principal, school administrator, art judge, and university professor in Mississippi. She enjoys creating artwork herself and with children. Contact: jjmoore@olemiss.edu

Made in the USA
Columbia, SC
19 April 2025